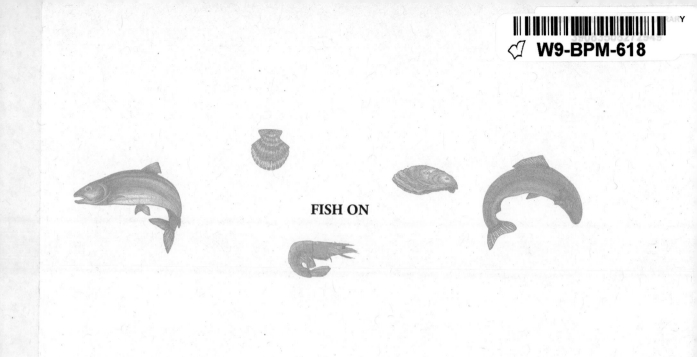

FISH ON

Fish On

SEAFOOD DISHES THAT MAKE A SPLASH

INGRID BAIER

TouchWood
Editions

TouchWood Editions
www.touchwoodeditions.com

Library and Archives Canada Cataloguing in Publication
Baier, Ingrid, 1967–
    Fish on : seafood dishes that make a splash / Ingrid Baier.

Includes index.
ISBN 978-1-926741-12-3
    1. Cookery (Seafood). 2. Cookery (Fish). I. Title.

TX747.B333 2010   641.6'92   C2010-903677-8

Editor: Holland Gidney
Cover illustrations: Debbie Harding
Interior illustrations by Ingrid Baier: pages 9, 11, 13, 15, 17–18, 20, 23, 25, 27, 29, 33,
37, 40, 42, 45, 47, 49, 53, 55, 57, 61, 63, 66, 71, 77, 80, 85, 88–89, 93–94, 98, 105, 107,
110, 115, 117,119, 123–124, 127, 129, 131, 133, 135, 138, 141 144, 146, 153, 155
Interior illustrations by Debbie Harding: pages i, iv, vii, 2, 5, 35, 51, 65, 69, 75, 79, 82,
87, 91, 95, 97, 101–102 ,109, 113, 137, 149–150, 157–158, 161, 164–165, 168
Cover design: Pete Kohut
Author photo: Ted Baier

 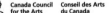

We gratefully acknowledge the financial support for our publishing activities
from the Government of Canada through the Canada Book Fund, Canada
Council for the Arts, and the province of British Columbia through the
British Columbia Arts Council and the Book Publishing Tax Credit.

Mixed Sources
Cert no. SW-COC-001271
© 1996 FSC
FSC

The interior pages of this book have been printed on 100% post-consumer
recycled paper, processed chlorine free, and printed with vegetable-based inks.

1 2 3 4 5 13 12 11 10

PRINTED IN CANADA

For Ted

Table of Contents

Introduction

This is not a book for food snobs. You will not find hand-foraged elderflower blossoms from the French Alps, unpasteurized ewe's milk from the Basque region of Spain, or Malaga raisins from Andalucia in any of my ingredient lists. Nor will you need a vacuum marinator, an espuma, or a copper cassoulet to prepare these recipes. I didn't write this book to establish my gastro-credence or to impress anyone with my culinary cachet—in fact, I'm not sure I have either. What I do have is a deep appreciation for the ocean and its bounty, both in the kitchen and out on the water.

I grew up on the north end of Vancouver Island, where I spent many happy summers fishing and preparing my own catch. I learned that cleaning crab before you cook it makes for a better crab feast. I learned that mishandling rockfish can lead to infected fingers. And I learned that there are few things as magnificent as a bald eagle as he swoops down to collect the undersize salmon you just released back into the water—almost taking your head off in the process. Growing up, seafood was simply part of my life, something absorbed by osmosis, not learned at a culinary institute. Not to knock cooking schools— they are, after all, the professionals, and I am always happy to follow meaningful expert advice. What I am *not* happy to follow is the trend of gastronomic one-upmanship that I see all around me in my everyday foodie life. With the evolution of the arch foodie and the trend towards using ever more esoteric ingredients and gadgets, I think it's time we get down off our culinary high-horses and start eating food because we like it—not because it costs nine hundred dollars an ounce, or because no one else on our street knows where to source edible gold foil. It's time we stop making co-workers feel gauche because they don't own a Rösle truffle slicer, and it would never occur to them to fluff their cappuccino foam with powdered tree bark. We need to look at the bigger picture and remember what's really important in life. Great sex is important. Good food with good friends is important. Decent merlot under forty bucks is important. Poaching your salmon in a tin-lined, hand-hammered copper fish kettle is . . . well, not important.

This book is meant as a reminder that "good" and "complicated" aren't synonyms. It's a reminder to eat what you like, and to like what you eat. Experiment. Don't be afraid to break the rules. I've never been a run-to-the-store-to-buy-one-ingredient kind of person, and these recipes evolved from my use-whatever's-in-the-fridge approach to cooking. So go ahead and try your favorite steak marinade on salmon steaks and your to-die-for grilling glaze on halibut. We're talking about your kitchen, not a chemistry lab. For every home cook who has ever been intimidated by seafood, this book is a call to foster your own tastes and honour your own opinions . . . and if they differ from the aficionados and the connoisseurs? Just remember, there's no such thing as the food police.

—Ingrid Baier

Sustainable Seafood

Unless you actually live right on the coast, it's impossible to subscribe to the locavore movement and still eat seafood. I moved to Alberta nearly 10 years ago (courtesy of the RCMP, who transferred my husband), which presented a real dilemma in terms of responsibly sourcing saltwater fish and seafood. Even on the Prairies, however, there are better and worse choices—both in terms of the fish we buy and where we buy it. Even if your salmon isn't caught within a 100-mile radius, there is usually a fish shop nearby—and shopping locally is the next best thing to sourcing locally.

Regardless of where you live, though, there are still some species that should never be purchased—either because they have been overfished to the point of near-extinction, or because the harvest method is too damaging to the environment or other marine life (dredging the ocean floor and drift nets spring immediately to mind). In our Web-based world, it is relatively easy for consumers to educate themselves regarding the state of our oceans, and to choose their seafood accordingly.

Sustainable Seafood Canada, a coalition comprised of the Canadian Parks and Wilderness Society, the Living Oceans Society, the Ecology Action Centre, the Sierra Club, and the David Suzuki Foundation, monitors the state of commercially harvested fish around the world and sponsors a regularly updated, user-friendly website that can help Canadians to make informed decisions: www.seachoice.org.

Basic Cooking Methods for Seafood

The common means of heat transfer used for cooking fish are steaming, poaching, roasting (or baking), sautéing, grilling, deep-frying, and grilling (or broiling).

Steaming

Seafood is steamed by suspending it above a boiling liquid. The most common steaming liquid is water, but starting with a small amount of a flavoured liquid, such as wine, and allowing it to reduce as it boils, will concentrate the flavours and create a good basis for many sauces. The seafood will drip juices into the wine as it cooks, which will intensify the flavour. This method is commonly used to cook shellfish (including mussels, oysters, clams, and crabs).

Poaching

Poaching is not the same as boiling, although both methods involve submerging food in a hot liquid. Although crab and lobster are sometimes boiled, for the most part, the heat and agitation from a rolling boil will break down the proteins and fats in seafood, leaving you with overcooked, mushy, and all-around-unappetizing fish.

To poach scallops or small fillets of fish—which take only a few minutes to cook—bring 1 to 2 inches (2.5 to 5 cm) of liquid to a gentle simmer, and then add the fish. To poach a whole fish, start with a cold liquid, and bring the liquid to a low simmer only after the fish has been added—starting with hot liquid will result in uneven cooking, and the outside of the fish will be overcooked by the time the inside is done.

Do not be intimidated by the idea of poaching a whole fish because you don't own a bona fide fish poacher. If you were lucky enough to have received a fish kettle for a wedding present, you can poach the fish on the stovetop. If not, you can use a heavy-duty turkey roaster and poach it in the oven (and if you don't own a turkey roaster, you can always wrap the fish in foil with a few sprigs of fresh thyme or a bay leaf and bake it in a slow oven; the result will be practically the same). There are really only three absolutes when it comes to poaching a whole fish: don't buy a fish that won't fit in your oven, never boil your fish, and avoid getting hung up on a lot of "shoulds"—you likely have enough of those in your life already!

Roasting or Baking

Roasting and baking both transfer heat through the dry air of an oven, although roasting uses both the top and bottom heating elements, and is generally understood to involve the higher temperatures that facilitate browning reactions in meat, whereas baking uses only the lower element and is often associated with the lower temperatures that produce cakes and cookies. Baking and roasting are commonly used to cook fillets, steaks, and whole fish. Pan-roasting (where a fillet is started on the stovetop and finished in a very hot oven) works very well with salmon.

Sautéing

Essentially, sautéing is synonymous with pan-frying, and involves stovetop cooking in just enough fat for the food to brown on the outside. As the food cooks, it drips juice into the pan; in turn, the water evaporates from the juice, and the remaining sugars and proteins caramelize onto the food's surface. When the food is removed from the pan and liquid (usually wine, stock or cream) is poured over the caramelized solids left behind (a process called "deglazing"), the reconstituted sugars and proteins form the basis of many sauces, including traditional pan gravies.

When pan-frying, be aware that some non-stick cookware can release toxic fumes when heated above 400°F (200°C). For those recipes that require you to sauté seafood on high heat, use a "seasoned" cast-iron frying pan. To season your pan, brush the inside of it liberally with cooking oil, and then heat it to very hot, but not smoking (the fumes from burning oil are also toxic). Allow the pan to cool for about 10 minutes, and then wipe it out with a dry rag. Over time, your frying pan will develop a barrier that will release fried foods almost as well as a non-stick skillet.

Deep-frying

When deep-frying seafood, it is important not to overload your pan. Too much cold seafood in a pan will lower the temperature of the oil to the point where the water will not evaporate. When this happens, your food will not sear, but poach in its own juice. Sautéing is commonly used to cook fish steaks, fillets, scallops, and prawns.

Deep-fried seafood is usually battered, and then completely submerged in very hot oil to instantly create a seal around the food. There are a couple of things to keep in mind when deep-frying at home. Whether you use an electric fryer, or an oil-filled pan on the stovetop, you have nowhere near the capacity of commercial fryers; home cooks will have greater success cooking small pieces of fish in small batches. Using smaller fillets not only prevents your fish from

sticking but, as with sautéing, overloading the oil with cold, wet food reduces its temperature, resulting in greasy, soggy batter. To fry effectively (which means absorbing as little oil into your food as possible), your oil must remain very hot. For this reason, you must use oil that can withstand high temperatures without breaking down (or igniting in your fryer), such as safflower, canola, or peanut oil. Deep-frying is commonly used for battered fish fillets and prawns.

Grilling or Broiling

Grilling, although usually done on a barbecue, is not the same as barbecuing. Barbecuing often involves tough cuts of meat, long cooking times, and the addition of smoke (think pulled pork), whereas grilling involves quickly searing the seafood (usually on both sides) over hot coals. Broiling involves searing the food under close, direct heat in the oven—the primary distinction between the two methods is the orientation of the food to the heat. Fish fillets, steaks, prawns, scallops, clams, mussels, and oysters on the half shell can all be grilled or broiled.

Crab and Lobster

About Crab

The most commonly harvested crab of the Pacific Northwest is the Dungeness, and it is commercially harvested from the British Columbia coast year-round and shipped all across Canada. The meat from the legs and claws ("lump" meat) is firm and sweet, with light pink streaks, while the body meat found just inside the topshell is similar in taste but paler and more delicate in texture. Dungeness is currently rated by Sustainable Seafood Canada as one of the best crab choices both in terms of environmental impact and sustainable fishing.

Buy your crab live from a reputable fishmonger with high turnover and clean tanks. Try to buy your crab as close to dinnertime as possible, but if you absolutely must buy it in advance, cover it with a damp towel and store it in the coldest part of your fridge for up to one day.

Your crab should not only be alive, it should be fairly active (although super-chilled water will make it sluggish), and it should feel heavy for its size. Crabs moult, so if the crab seems too light, it may not have had the chance to grow into its new shell yet. Extra-large crabs (2 pounds [1 kilogram] or more) may mean less work to shell, but smaller crabs (1 to 1½ pounds [500 to 750 grams]) will have a sweeter flavour and finer muscle texture.

If the crabs are in the same tank as the lobsters, one way to gauge overall freshness is to check out the antennae on the lobsters: they should be long and intact. Crustaceans are cannibalistic and lobsters that have been in a tank together for a long time will have eaten off each other's antennae.

Killing and Cleaning Crab

Once a crab has been killed, the flesh deteriorates rapidly as the digestive enzymes of the liver begin to break down the proteins in the surrounding muscle tissue. Consequently, do not kill your crab until you are ready to cook it. Their short shelf life prompts many people to drop crabs into boiling water while they are still alive. Please don't do this. Dropping a live crab into a rolling boil will literally cook the taste of the viscera into the flesh, sully the cooking liquid (which will inevitably leak out of the shell and onto your plate while you're eating), cause the meat to become waterlogged and, when served intact, make the meal significantly more labour-intensive for your dinner guests.

Eating crab directly from the shell is, by definition, messy—but fresh Dungeness should be the chin-dripping-finger-food kind of messy, not the crab-guts-sitting-in-a-slough-of-brackish-water kind of messy. Fortunately, you can avoid said mess simply by killing and cleaning the crab prior to cooking.

Crabs can be killed easily and swiftly with a single, sharp blow to the abdomen. Simply place the crab on its back in your kitchen sink and tap sharply against the thin, narrow undershell with a mallet or small hammer. The blow should be hard enough to break through the undershell, but not so hard that it breaks the crab in half and cracks the topshell. This will kill the crab instantly.

Once you have killed the crab, turn it onto its abdomen and hold the legs on one side firmly with one hand. With your other hand, pry or twist off the topshell, being careful not to break it. As the shell comes off, the crab legs will fall naturally into two "halves," and most of the viscera will remain inside the topshell. If you are saving the shells for presentation purposes, shake out the innards and discard them, before giving the shells a good wash under cold running water.

The "body" meat will remain attached to the tops of the legs, still encased in a translucent layer of shell. Sometimes the gills will stick to the top of this meat;

if this happens, simply peel them off and discard. After you rinse the crab halves well under cold running water, they are ready for cooking.

This method is even easier if you have two people: have one person hold the legs while the other holds the shell and twists.

About Lobster

Lobster, like crab, should be bought live on the day you plan to cook it from a reputable fishmonger with high turnover and clean tanks. A lobster should flip its tail vigorously when picked up, and its antennae should be mostly intact. Crustaceans are cannibalistic and lobsters that have been in a tank together for an extended period of time will have eaten off each other's antennae. Live lobsters and crabs are often packaged in waxed cardboard boxes, and, if necessary, you can store the lobster in this box in the coldest part of your fridge for up to one day.

A lobster in its prime will be feisty, so make sure that the rubber bands on its claws are intact before you pick it up. Believe it or not, a pinch from a lobster can send you to the ER for multiple stitches—some estimates put the crushing force of a lobster claw on a human finger as high as 1,180 pounds per square inch.

Expert opinions of chefs and biologists alike vary as to the virtue of dropping a live lobster into boiling water. Lobsters have extremely primitive nervous systems that do not actually include brains *per se*, but a collection of ganglion for each body segment, which makes it difficult to pinpoint the location of their pain processor (or even to state with certainty whether or not they have one). Erring on the humane side, however, means killing your lobster *before* you cook it.

The first step is to anaesthetize the lobster by putting it in the freezer for 15 minutes prior to killing it. Afterwards, place the chilled lobster on several layers of paper towels laid on top of a large cutting board and hold it flat by the tail with your non-dominant hand. Using your dominant hand, insert a large, sharp chef's knife into the base of the head and push all the way down. Lever the knife towards your dominant side, splitting the lobster's head in half and effectively killing it.

When cleaning lobster for stuffing, scoop everything out of the head cavity and discard it. Many lobster aficionados eat the liver (called the tomalley) as a delicacy, but I could never see the appeal of eating the filter organ of a bottom feeder. Call me unsophisticated . . . (Hey, I heard that.)

Spiny and Caribbean lobsters trap-harvested off the US Atlantic and Florida coasts are the best choice in terms of sustainable seafood.

Steamed Dungeness "Halves" with Champagne Vanilla Butter

2 live Dungeness crabs, about 1 ½ lb (750 g) each

Champagne Vanilla Butter

½ cup (125 mL) champagne

half a vanilla bean

¼ cup (60 mL) unsalted butter, at room temperature

Serves 2.

Wine Suggestion: Champagne

Many cooks (and restaurants) will simply drop live a Dungeness into boiling water and serve the whole crab on a platter along with a claw cracker and a shellfish knife. Steaming cleaned crab halves over a salted water, broth, or wine, however, results in sweeter, more succulent flesh and creates an altogether more pleasant dining experience. And, because the shells are preserved and the crabs reassembled prior to serving, killing and cleaning the crab beforehand need not compromise presentation.

1. Being careful not to break the topshells, kill and clean the crabs (p. 7). Reserve the shells, clean them, and boil them, in a separate pan, for 5 minutes. Drain and set aside.
2. Steam the crab halves until the claw shells turn red and the meat is white and opaque, about 5 to 7 minutes, depending on the size of your crabs.
3. Remove the crab halves from the steamer and match up the mates. Place the halves side by side on two plates and set the cooked topshells back on top of the crab halves. *Voila!* You have freshly steamed "whole" Dungeness crabs, without the mess and the waste! Serve immediately with Champagne Vanilla Butter.

Champagne Vanilla Butter

1. In a small saucepan on high heat, bring the champagne to a boil. Slice the vanilla bean half lengthwise to expose the seeds and add it to the champagne. Reduce the heat to medium and simmer until the liquid is reduced by half.
2. Remove the vanilla pod halves and scrape the seeds into the reduction. Discard the pods.

3. Whisk the butter into the reduction 1 tablespoon (15 mL) at a time, whisking constantly until the butter is fully incorporated and the mixture starts to thicken, about 3 minutes. Remove from heat and allow to cool slightly. Pour into 2 small dipping bowls and serve with freshly steamed crab.

Easy Garlic Butter

6 garlic cloves
¼ cup (60 mL) unsalted butter

Champagne Vanilla Butter is quite sweet, so if you prefer a more savoury butter, substitute the following sauce.

1. Squash the garlic cloves with the side of large chef's knife to pop them out of their skins, and then squash them a few more times to release the oils (don't bother chopping—you won't be eating the garlic, just infusing the butter with its flavour).
2. Melt the butter in a small saucepan on low heat (or, alternately, melt it in a glass measuring cup in the microwave), and then add the garlic.
3. Turn off the heat and allow the butter to sit for about 10 minutes for the flavour to develop. If it starts to solidify, simply re-melt the butter just before serving and transfer it to 2 small dipping bowls. Serve with lemon wedges alongside freshly steamed crab.

Cold Crab Rolls with Tarragon Mayonnaise

Traditional New England lobster rolls bind chunks of fresh lobster meat inside a hotdog bun using herbed mayonnaise dressing, but they are just as delicious when made with fresh steamed Dungeness crab and served in a fresh baguette.

Mayonnaise Dressing

2 Tbsp (30 mL) mayonnaise

½ Tbsp (7.5 mL) minced fresh tarragon

1 Tbsp (15 mL) minced red onion

1 Tbsp (15 mL) minced green onion

1 tsp (5 mL) freshly squeezed lime juice

¼ tsp (1 mL) salt

freshly ground pepper, to taste

Crab Rolls

1 live Dungeness crab

1 tsp (5 mL) dried tarragon

1 fresh baguette

2 Tbsp (30 mL) unsalted butter, at room temperature

Serves 2.

Wine Suggestion: Chardonnay

Mayonnaise Dressing

1. In a small, non-reactive mixing bowl, combine all the ingredients. Cover with plastic wrap and refrigerate.

Crab Rolls

1. Kill and clean the crab (p. 7), discarding the topshell. In a large, covered pan, bring 2 inches (5 cm) of water to a boil and add the tarragon. Add the crab halves and poach until the claw shells turn bright red and the meat is opaque, about 5 to 7 minutes.

2. When the crab is cool enough to handle, about 5 minutes, remove all the meat, including the white body meat. Chop it into bite-size pieces and set aside to cool.

3. Allow the crabmeat to cool for another 10 minutes, and then fold it into the Mayonnaise Dressing. Cover with plastic wrap and refrigerate for at least 30 minutes.

4. Cut two 5-inch (12 cm) loaves from the baguette. Slice open the tops and scoop out an inch (2.5 cm) of bread to make room for the crab. Spread the softened butter over the tops of the bread and pan-fry on medium heat in a cast-iron frying pan until browned, about 2 minutes.

5. Divide the crab mixture evenly between the 2 toasted loaves and serve immediately.

Easy Curried Crab Legs

When poaching crab in any kind of flavourful sauce, use a rolling pin to gently crack the shells prior to cooking. Doing so will give the sauce a chance to penetrate the crab, resulting in more flavourful meat.

1. Kill and clean the crabs (p. 7), discarding the shells. Separate the claws and legs, leaving the body meat at the top of each shell intact.
2. In a wide pan large enough to hold the crab legs, melt the butter on medium heat. Whisk in the curry powder and cook until fragrant, about 2 minutes. Whisk in the coconut milk and the jalapeno, stirring to make a smooth paste. Bring the sauce to a simmer.
3. Add the cracked crab legs and stir well to evenly coat the crab. Cover and simmer, stirring every minute or so, until the crab shells turn bright red and the meat is white and opaque, about 8 to 10 minutes, depending on the size of your crabs.

2 live Dungeness crabs
2 Tbsp (30 mL) butter
2 Tbsp (30 mL) curry powder
1 jalapeno pepper, seeded and chopped
1 12-oz (355 mL) can coconut milk
Serves 2.

Wine Suggestion: Pinot Gris

Hot Crab Rolls with Butter Beer

For this hot variation, you start by poaching the crab in the beer, and then use the leftover poaching liquid to make the sauce.

Crab Rolls

1 live Dungeness crab

¾ cup (185 mL) of your favourite beer (preferably lager)

1 fresh baguette

2 Tbsp (30 mL) unsalted butter, at room temperature

Butter Beer

½ cup (125 mL) liquid from poaching crab

1 Tbsp (15 mL) minced white onion

¼ tsp (1 mL) dried thyme

¼ tsp (1 mL) salt

freshly ground pepper, to taste (white if you have it)

⅛ tsp (0.5 mL) pure vanilla extract

¼ cup (60 mL) unsalted butter, at room temperature

Serves 2.

Beer Suggestion: Cold lager

1. Kill and clean the crab (p. 7), discarding the topshell.
2. In a medium saucepan, bring the beer to a simmer and add the crab directly to the liquid. Poach until the claw shells turn bright red and the meat is white and opaque, about 8 to 10 minutes, depending on the size of your crab.
3. Remove the crab from the poaching liquid and set it aside to cool. Keep the poaching liquid for the Butter Beer.
4. Strain the poaching liquid through a fine sieve into a small saucepan and bring it to a boil on high heat. Add the onion, thyme, salt, and pepper. Reduce the heat to medium-low and simmer until reduced by half. Whisk in the vanilla. Add the butter 1 tablespoon (15 mL) at a time, whisking constantly until all the butter is incorporated and the sauce has thickened, about 3 to 4 minutes. Remove from heat while you shell the crab.
5. Use a rolling pin to gently crack the claws and legs. Remove all the meat, including the white body meat, leaving it in large pieces.
6. Cut two 6-inch (15 cm) loaves from the baguette and butterfly them by slicing open the top and scooping out an inch (2.5 cm) of bread to make more room for the crab. Spread the softened butter over the tops of the bread and pan-fry in a cast-iron frying pan until browned, about 2 minutes.

7. While the bread is frying, reheat the Butter Beer on medium heat, whisking until it just starts to simmer, about 1 minute. Add the crabmeat directly to the sauce and heat through, about 1 minute.
8. Divide the crab mixture between the 2 toasted loaves and serve immediately.

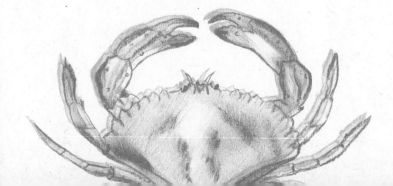

Crab-stuffed Lobster

I first ate crab-stuffed lobster more than 15 years ago, following my husband's impromptu proposal on a Maui beach. After a hectic afternoon spent looking for a Justice of the Peace (a vagabond we found sleeping on the beach agreed to be our witness), we stood ankle-deep in the surf to exchange our vows. Dinner that night seemed to warrant something extra-special; so, ignoring the exorbitant price, I ordered the crab-stuffed lobster. I have since recreated my own version of this dish at least once a year, either for Valentine's Day, or a week later, on our anniversary.

Crab Stuffing

1 live Dungeness crab

4 green onions, finely chopped

1 garlic clove, minced

2 Tbsp (30 mL) chopped cilantro

3 Tbsp (45 mL) freshly squeezed lime juice

3 Tbsp (45 mL) mayonnaise

Lobster

2 live lobsters, about 1½ lb (750 g) each

1 cup (250 mL) dry white wine

3 Tbsp (45 mL) melted unsalted butter, for brushing

2 Tbsp (30 mL) fine dry breadcrumbs

Serves 2.

Wine Suggestion: Champagne

Crab Stuffing

1. Kill and clean the crab (p. 7), discarding the topshell. Steam the crab halves until the shells turn bright red, and the meat is white and opaque, about 5 to 7 minutes, depending on the size of your crab. Remove from the steamer and set aside to cool.
2. In a small, non-reactive mixing bowl, combine the green onion, garlic, cilantro, lime juice, and mayonnaise.
3. When the crab is cool enough to handle, after about 5 minutes, use a rolling pin to gently crack the claws and legs. Remove all the meat, saving the white body meat for another recipe (see the "Leftovers" chapter for ideas). Fold the remaining lump crabmeat into the mayonnaise mixture and set aside while you cook the lobsters.

Lobster

1. Kill the lobsters (p. 9). In a covered pan large enough to hold both lobsters, bring the wine to a high simmer, add the lobsters, and poach them for about 4 minutes.

2. Remove the lobsters from the poaching liquid. They will already be partly split from when you killed them but when they are cool enough to handle, after about 3 or 4 minutes, split them the rest of the way lengthwise so you have 4 halves. Scoop out and discard everything you find in the head cavity.

3. Preheat the barbecue to medium (400°F [200°C]). Scrape and oil the grill, and then increase the heat to high (500°F [260°C]). Brush the lobster meat with the melted butter and grill the lobsters, shell side up, until the shells turn red, about 4 minutes.

4. Turn the lobsters and fill the head cavities with the Crab Stuffing. Brush the meat and stuffing with the melted butter again, sprinkling with breadcrumbs this time. Grill until the lobster is fully cooked and the crab stuffing is heated through, about 4 minutes.

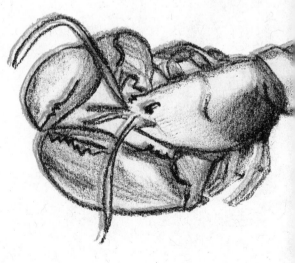

Crab-encrusted Halibut

The addition of the crab crust adds elegance to an already delicious fish.

1 live Dungeness crab
1 cup (250 mL) Panko breadcrumbs
1 cup (250 mL) freshly grated Parmesan cheese
1 Tbsp (15 mL) minced fresh tarragon
⅓ cup (80 mL) melted unsalted butter
4 5-oz (150 g) halibut fillets
1 tsp (5 mL) butter, for greasing
4 sprigs fresh tarragon, for garnishing
Serves 4.

Wine Suggestion: Sauvignon Blanc

1. Kill and clean the crab (p. 7), discarding the topshells. Steam the crab halves until the shells turn bright red and the meat is white and opaque, about 5 to 7 minutes, depending on the size of your crab. Remove the crab from the steamer and set aside to cool.
2. When the crab is cool enough to handle, after about 5 minutes, use a rolling pin to gently crack the claws and legs. Remove all the meat and set it aside. Leave the lump meat in large pieces (save the body meat for another recipe; see the "Leftovers" chapter for ideas).
3. Preheat the oven to 400°F (200°C).
4. In a medium mixing bowl, combine the breadcrumbs, Parmesan, and tarragon. Drizzle in the butter a little at a time, stirring well to evenly coat the breadcrumbs.
5. Rinse the halibut fillets and dry well using paper towels. Grease a baking sheet with butter and place the halibut directly on it. Spread a quarter of the crab mixture evenly over each halibut fillet. Bake on the middle rack until done, 10 minutes cooking time for each inch of thickness. Serve immediately.

Baked Crab and Artichoke Dip

Served as a starter with toasted baguette rounds, this succulent dip is the absolute best way to stretch a single Dungeness between four people.

1. Kill and clean the crab (p. 7), discarding the topshell. Steam the crab halves until the claw shells turn bright red and the meat is white and opaque, about 5 to 7 minutes, depending on the size of your crab. Remove the crab from the steamer and allow it to cool.

2. When the crab is cool enough to handle, after about 5 minutes, use a rolling pin to gently crack the claws and legs. Remove all the meat (including the body meat) and set it aside.

3. Preheat the oven to 400°F (200°C). Rinse and chop the artichoke hearts, squeezing the pieces dry with paper towels.

4. In a medium saucepan on medium heat, melt the butter and sauté the onion, garlic, salt, and pepper until fragrant (do not brown), about 3 minutes. Stir in the white wine, mustard, and Tabasco, and then whisk in the cream. Simmer the mixture until slightly thickened, about 2 to 3 minutes. Gradually add the Gruyère, whisking constantly until the cheese is melted and the sauce is smooth.

5. Transfer the sauce to a baking dish and gently fold in the artichoke hearts and crabmeat. Sprinkle the Parmesan overtop and bake the dip, uncovered, until the cheese is golden brown, about 15 to 20 minutes. Sprinkle with the tarragon and serve piping hot with toasted baguette rounds

1 live Dungeness crab

1 12-oz (355 mL) jar artichoke hearts

1 Tbsp (15 mL) unsalted butter

2 Tbsp (30 mL) minced white onion

1 garlic clove, minced

½ tsp (2 mL) salt

freshly ground pepper, to taste

2 Tbsp (30 mL) dry white wine

1 tsp (5 mL) Dijon mustard

1 tsp (5 mL) Tabasco sauce

½ cup (125 mL) whipping cream

½ cup (125 mL) grated Gruyère cheese

¼ cup (60 mL) freshly grated Parmesan cheese

2 Tbsp (30 mL) minced fresh tarragon, for garnishing

Serves 4 as a starter.

Crab Cakes

Crab cakes made from large chunks of freshly steamed Dungeness (lump meat only) make a truly sumptuous starter for a formal dinner party. Serve them with Herbed Mayonnaise Dip (p. 21) or aioli.

Crab Cakes

2 live Dungeness crabs

1 Tbsp (15 mL) unsalted butter

1 garlic clove, minced

2 Tbsp (10 mL) minced shallot

3 Tbsp (15 mL) minced red bell pepper

¼ cup (60 mL) Blender Mayonnaise (p. 21)

1 Tbsp (15 mL) freshly squeezed lime juice

1 tsp (5 mL) Worcestershire sauce

½ tsp (2 mL) dried mustard

1 tsp (5 mL) minced parsley

½ tsp (2 mL) sea salt

freshly ground pepper, to taste

1½ cup (250 mL) fine dry breadcrumbs, divided

1 egg

¼ cup (60 mL) canola oil, for frying

Serves 8 as a starter.

Wine Suggestion: Unoaked Chardonnay

Crab Cakes

1. Preheat the oven to 350°F (180°C). Kill and clean the crab (p. 7), discarding the topshell. Steam the crab halves until the claw shells turn bright red, and the meat is white and opaque, about 5 to 7 minutes, depending on the size of your crab. Remove from the steamer and set aside to cool.

2. When the crab is cool enough to handle, about 5 minutes, use a rolling pin to gently crack the claws and legs. Remove all the lump meat and drain it on paper towels (save the white body meat for another recipe; see the "Leftovers" chapter for ideas).

3. In a small frying pan, melt the butter on medium heat and sauté the garlic, shallot, and red pepper until they soften (do not brown), about 4 minutes. Remove from the heat and set aside to cool completely.

4. In a medium mixing bowl, whisk together the mayonnaise, lime juice, Worcestershire sauce, dried mustard, parsley, salt, and pepper. Add the cooled shallot mixture, and then stir in ½ cup (125 mL) of the breadcrumbs. Gently fold in the crabmeat.

5. In a small bowl, whisk the egg until light and fluffy, and then fold it into the crab mixture. Divide the crab mixture into small balls, about 2 inches (5 cm) in diameter.

6. Spread the remaining breadcrumbs on a plate, and gently roll each ball in the crumbs, coating well. Gently flatten each crab ball to make a "cake." Prepare all the cakes before cooking.

7. Preheat the oven to 200 F (93°C). In a non-stick frying pan, heat half of the oil on high heat and cook the crab cakes a few at a time since adding too many to the pan at once will drop the temperature and the cakes will not be crisp. Cook on both sides until golden brown, about 4 minutes per side. Keep the first batch hot in the oven while you finish frying all the cakes, adding more oil to the pan as needed.
8. When all the cakes are cooked, serve them piping hot with the Herbed Mayonnaise Dip or aioli on the side.

Blender Mayonnaise

1. In a blender on high speed, process the egg yolks, dried mustard, and cayenne pepper until fully combined.
2. With the motor still running, remove the inner lid and, very slowly, in a thin stream, pour in the olive oil. Continue to blend on medium speed until the mixture thickens.
3. Add the salt and the lemon juice and blend to combine.

Herbed Mayonnaise Dip

1. Whisk together all the ingredients; cover and refrigerate until needed.

Blender Mayonnaise

2 egg yolks, at room temperature
1 tsp (5 mL) dried mustard
¼ tsp (1 mL) cayenne pepper
1 cup (250 mL) olive oil
1 tsp (5 mL) salt
1 Tbsp (15 mL) freshly squeezed lemon juice
Makes about 1 cup (250 mL).

Herbed Mayonnaise Dip

½ cup (125 mL) Blender Mayonnaise
1 garlic clove, minced
½ tsp (2 mL) Worcestershire sauce
1 tsp (5 mL) minced fresh tarragon
1 tsp (5 mL) minced fresh basil
Makes about ½ cup (125 mL).

Crab Thermidor

Although the traditional version of this recipe calls for lobster, it is a delicious way to enjoy fresh Dungeness. It's also a perfect meal for an anniversary or Valentine's Day. After all, there is no better way to say "I love you" than "*See?* I shelled your crab legs for you . . ."

2 live Dungeness crabs
2 Tbsp (30 mL) unsalted butter
1 shallot, minced
2 Tbsp (30 mL) flour
¾ cup (185 mL) milk
½ tsp (2 mL) salt
freshly ground pepper, to taste
(white if you have it)
¼ tsp (1 mL) ground nutmeg
¼ tsp (1 mL) cayenne
1 Tbsp (15 mL) minced fresh tarragon
1 egg yolk
3 Tbsp (45 mL) whipping cream
2 Tbsp (30 mL) freshly grated Parmesan
2 Tbsp (30 mL) grated Gruyère

Serves 2.

Wine Suggestion: Chardonnay (unless it's your anniversary, in which case you may want to go with blanc de blancs Champagne)

1. Being careful not to break the topshells, kill and clean the crabs (p. 7). Retain the shells, removing any innards stuck to the insides; rinse them and cook them in a pot of boiling water for 5 minutes. Drain the shells and set aside.
2. Steam the crab halves until the shells turn red and the meat is white and opaque, about 5 to 7 minutes, depending on the size of your crabs. Remove the crabs from the steamer and set aside.
3. When the crabs are cool enough to handle, after about 3 or 4 minutes, use a rolling pin to gently crack the claws and legs. Remove all the meat and place the lump meat in a mixing bowl (save the white body meat for another recipe; see the "Leftovers" chapter for ideas).
4. Preheat the oven to 400°F (200°C).
5. In a small saucepan, melt the butter on medium heat and add the shallot. Sauté until the shallot is translucent. Whisk in the flour and cook for 2 to 3 minutes (do not allow to brown).
6. Gradually whisk in the milk, and then add the salt, pepper, nutmeg, cayenne, and tarragon. Bring the milk to a simmer, and then turn off the heat and allow it to cool long enough for the temperature to drop by about 20°F (11°C), about 3 minutes.

The temperature must be under 180°F (82°C) when you add the egg or the yolk will scramble. (Set the pan in a bowl of ice water if you're in a hurry, and check the temperature with a candy thermometer if you're in a panic.)

7. In a small mixing bowl, beat the egg yolk into the whipping cream, and then whisk this mixture into the sauce. Continue whisking until the sauce thickens, about 2 minutes. Pour half the sauce into the mixing bowl with the crabmeat and stir to blend, being careful not to break up the crabmeat.

8. Spoon the crabmeat/sauce mixture into the cooked crab shells, topping with the remaining sauce, and then sprinkle the whole thing with the grated cheeses.

9. Bake for 5 minutes to heat the crab through, and then switch the oven to broil and grill until the cheese topping is golden brown, about 1 to 2 minutes. Serve piping hot.

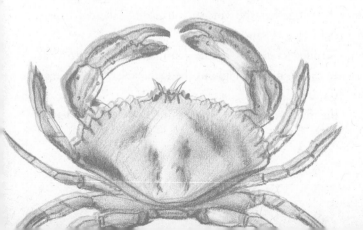

Chilled Marinated Crab Legs

Cold, marinated crab legs, served with a couple of contrasting dipping sauces, are a great make-ahead dish for a party when hot Dungeness halves simply aren't feasible. Even though the legs are partially cracked ahead of time, serve the crab with claw crackers and seafood picks.

Crab

4 live Dungeness crabs

crushed ice, for serving

Cooked Crab Marinade

1 cup (250 mL) white wine vinegar

½ cup (125 mL) extra virgin olive oil

1 tsp (5 mL) Tabasco sauce

1 Tbsp (15 mL) capers, with juice

1 tsp (5 mL) Worcestershire sauce

3 garlic cloves, sliced

1 medium onion, thinly sliced

Serves 12 as buffet finger food.

Crab

1. Kill and clean the crabs (p. 7), discarding the topshells. Steam the crab halves until the shells turn bright red, and the meat is white and opaque, about 5 to 7 minutes, depending on the size of your crabs. Remove from the steamer and set aside to cool.
2. When the crabs are cool enough to handle, after about 5 minutes, snap the claws and legs off each body, saving the white body meat for another recipe (see the "Leftovers" chapter for ideas).
3. Use a rolling pin to gently crack the claws and legs but leave the meat inside the shells. Use a large colander to drain the cracked legs and claws for 5 minutes, and then transfer to a large bowl. Cover the bowl with plastic wrap and refrigerate for 3 hours.

Cooked Crab Marinade

1. In a mixing bowl large enough to hold all the crab legs and claws, whisk together the vinegar, olive oil, Tabasco, capers, Worcestershire sauce, and garlic.
2. Add the chilled crab legs to the marinade and stir to coat. Distribute the onions throughout the crab, cover, and refrigerate for 30 minutes, stirring occasionally.
3. Discard the marinade and the onions, and drain the crab legs in a colander.

4. To serve, choose a serving dish large enough to hold the crushed ice and the crab legs and claws (and one deep enough to keep the crab out of the water as the ice melts). Arrange the cracked crab on top of the ice and serve with homemade Tartar Sauce and Cocktail Sauce (p. 119).

Tartar Sauce

1. In a blender on high speed, process the egg yolks, dried mustard, and cayenne pepper until fully combined. With the motor still running, remove the inner lid and, very slowly, in a thin stream, pour in the olive oil. Continue to blend until the mixture has thickened. Add the salt and vinegar, and then blend to combine.

2. Transfer the mixture to a small mixing bowl and hand-whisk in the shallot and the relish. If using anchovy fillets, drain on paper towels, and then mash in a small bowl with the back of a fork. Stir this paste into the tartar sauce. Cover the sauce and refrigerate until needed.

Tartar Sauce

2 egg yolks, at room temperature

2 tsp (10 mL) dried mustard

¼ tsp (1 mL) cayenne pepper

1 cup (250 mL) olive oil (not extra virgin)

1 tsp (5 mL) salt

1 Tbsp plus 1 tsp (20 mL) white vinegar

1 shallot, minced

2 Tbsp (30 mL) sweet pickle relish

2 anchovy fillets (optional)

Makes about 1 cup (250 mL).

Crab Bisque

This creamy soup makes an elegant first course and is another terrific way to stretch one Dungeness between four people.

Crab Stock

1 live Dungeness crab

2 Tbsp (30 mL) unsalted butter

1 small carrot, diced

1 small onion, diced

1 stalk celery, diced

half a fennel bulb, diced

1 medium fresh tomato, diced

2 garlic cloves, minced

1 bay leaf

5 cups (1.25 litres) water

Serves 4.

Crab Stock

1. Kill and clean the crab (p. 7). Retain and clean the topshell. Steam the crab halves and the shell; set aside to cool.
2. When the crab is cool enough to handle, use a rolling pin to gently crack the claws and legs and remove all the meat from the crab, including the white body meat. Chop the meat into bite-size pieces and it set aside to add to the finished bisque. Cover and refrigerate until needed.
2. Chop the crab shell into medium pieces. In a large saucepan on medium heat, melt the butter and add the carrot, onion, celery, fennel, tomato, garlic, and bay leaf. Cook for 10 minutes, stirring occasionally, until the vegetables are softened (do not allow to brown). Add the shell pieces and the water and bring to a boil. Reduce heat to low, cover, and simmer for 1 hour.
3. Allow the mixture to cool to room temperature. In batches, transfer the stock, including the shell pieces, to a food processor and pulse until the shell is coarsely ground. When you have ground the entire batch, strain the stock through a fine sieve into a medium mixing bowl. Discard the shell pieces and vegetables.

Crab Bisque

1. In a medium saucepan, bring Crab Stock to a low boil. Stir in the brandy and the white wine.
2. Reduce the heat to medium-low, and then whisk in the cream and the lemon juice. Gently stir in the reserved crabmeat and heat through, about 1 to 2 minutes. Add the salt, pepper, and cayenne.
3. Ladle the bisque into 4 individual bowls, garnishing with Crème Fraîche if desired. Serve immediately.

Crème Fraîche

Crème fraîche, which is expensive to buy but easy to make, is thickened French cream that is often used plain, or blended with a mixture of fine herbs, for garnishing cream-based soups. Because crème fraîche takes about 24 hours to thicken, you will need to make it at least a day ahead, but it will keep for about a week in the fridge.

1. Combine the cream and buttermilk. Cover and let sit in a spot that is slightly warmer than room temperature for 24 hours. If the mixture has not thickened after 24 hours, move it to a warmer spot and let it sit for another 8 hours. (Don't worry about the cream spoiling; the *lactobacillus* culture in the buttermilk will "sour" the cream while inhibiting the growth of harmful bacteria.)

Crab Bisque

4 cups (1 L) Crab Stock
¼ cup (60 mL) brandy
¼ cup (60 mL) dry white wine
¼ cup (60 mL) whipping cream
1 Tbsp (15 mL) freshly squeezed lemon juice
reserved meat from 1 cooked Dungeness crab
½ tsp (2 mL) salt
freshly ground pepper, to taste
¼ tsp (1 mL) cayenne pepper
Crème Fraiche (p. 27), for garnishing (optional)

Crème Fraîche

2 cups (500 mL) whipping cream
¼ cup (60 mL) buttermilk
Makes about 2¼ cup (560 mL).

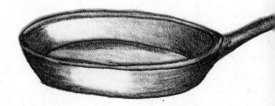

West Coast Jambalaya

Jambalaya is similar to paella in that both are single-pot, rice-based meals that incorporate the tradition of whatever-you-have-on-hand for the meat. In my bastardized West Coast version, I use the body meat from Dungeness crabs in the jambalaya itself and serve crab legs on top, still in the shell.

2 live Dungeness crabs

2 Tbsp (30 mL) unsalted butter

1 small onion, diced

3 garlic cloves, minced

1 tsp (5 mL) red pepper flakes

½ tsp (2 mL) cayenne pepper

1 tsp (5 mL) paprika

½ tsp (2 mL) dried thyme leaves

½ tsp (2 mL) dried basil

1 tsp (5 mL) sea salt

freshly ground black pepper, to taste

1 cup (250 mL) uncooked long-grain white rice

2 fresh medium tomatoes, blanched, peeled, and chopped (or substitute 1 14-oz [398 mL] can of good-quality whole plum tomatoes)

2 cups (500 mL) Fish Stock (p. 160) (or substitute chicken stock)

Serves 4.

Wine Suggestion: Off-dry Riesling or Muscat

1. Kill and clean the crabs (p. 7), discarding the topshells. Steam the crab halves until the shells turn bright red, and the meat is white and opaque, about 5 to 7 minutes, depending on the size of your crabs. Remove from the steamer and set aside to cool.

2. When the crabs are cool enough to handle, after about 5 minutes, remove the white body meat from each crab and set it aside. Leave the meat in the legs intact.

3. In a heavy-bottomed frying pan, melt the butter on medium heat and add the onions and garlic. Sauté until fragrant, about 3 minutes, and then add the red pepper flakes, cayenne pepper, paprika, thyme, basil, salt, and black pepper. Add the rice and cook until the rice turns translucent, about 3 minutes, stirring continuously.

4. Add the tomatoes and the stock to the rice mixture and bring the liquid to a boil. When most of the liquid has been absorbed, about 5 minutes, turn the heat down to very low, cover the pot, and cook for 10 minutes.

5. Gently fold in the crab body meat and set the crab legs on top. Re-cover and cook until the crab is heated through, about 5 more minutes. Serve immediately.

Crab Fettuccine
with Tarragon Butter

This recipe divides two crabs between four people, but the succulent taste and texture of fresh steamed Dungeness—unadulterated by a heavy cream sauce—still takes centre stage against the plain backdrop of lemony noodles.

1. Kill and clean the crabs (p. 7), discarding the topshells. Steam the crab halves until the claw shells turn bright red, and the meat is white and opaque, about 5 to 7 minutes, depending on the size of your crabs. Remove the crabs from the steamer and set aside to cool.

2. When the crabs are cool enough to handle, after 3 to 4 minutes, use a rolling pin to gently crack the claws and legs. Remove all the meat, including the body meat, and set it aside.

3. Bring a very large pot of salted water to a rolling boil. Add the fettuccine and cook until just done (fresh pasta will float to the top of the pot when it is cooked). Drain, but do not rinse. Transfer the noodles to a large bowl and toss with the lemon juice.

4. In a medium saucepan, melt the butter on medium heat; add the salt, pepper, and tarragon and sauté for 1 minute.

5. Add the crabmeat and cook until the crab is heated through, about 1 more minute. Divide the pasta equally between 4 pasta bowls, topping with the crab and garnishing with the tarragon sprigs. Serve immediately.

2 live Dungeness crabs
¾ lb (375 g) fresh fettuccine
(or dried, if you don't have fresh)
3 Tbsp (30 mL) freshly squeezed lemon juice
½ cup (125 mL) unsalted butter
½ tsp (2 mL) sea salt
freshly ground pepper, to taste
¼ cup (60 mL) finely chopped fresh tarragon
4 sprigs fresh tarragon, for garnishing
Serves 4.

Wine Suggestion: Chardonnay

Oysters, Mussels, and Clams

Oysters, mussels, and clams are all bivalves so the buying and storing guidelines are basically the same for all of them. As with any seafood, source these shellfish from a fishmonger or a grocery store with a high turnover; for the best results, buy your shellfish on the day you plan to eat it. Fresh bivalves must always be bought (and cooked) alive, so look for shellfish with tightly closed, unbroken shells. If the shell is open, tap on it: if the shell snaps shut, the animal inside is still alive. Due to a strong ligament at the hinge that acts as a spring and pulls the shells apart mechanically at the opposite end, the default position for bivalves is "open." In order to close its shell, the animal must be able to overcome this ligament by activating its adductor muscle—if it cannot, it is either dead or dying (do not buy it).

Conversely, heat causes the adductor muscle to relax so the shell will open again naturally during cooking. If it doesn't, the animal inside has probably been dead long enough for the "spring" to fail (which is why you should discard it).

If you cannot cook your bivalves on the day of purchase, they will last for a couple of days in the fridge. They keep best on a bed of ice, covered with a damp towel (the ice will need drainage or the ice-melt will drown your shellfish) but you can also store them covered with a damp cloth on a tray in the coldest part of the fridge. Mussels and oysters are intertidal creatures—inhabiting the beach area between high and low tide—which means they need periodic exposure to air and will die if you submerge them for too long in water or store them in an airtight plastic bag. In addition, oysters should always be stored cup-shaped shell down.

Bivalves that are farmed by suspended aquaculture are a best choice in terms of sustainability, but wild stocks are not over-fished at this time and are a great alternative for those West Coasters who want to harvest their own.

About Oysters

Because of their smaller size, commercially available mussels and clams are rarely shucked prior to cooking and are usually steamed, poached, or grilled in their shells. Oysters have a deep, cup-shaped bottom shell and a flat topshell, which increases your options for cooking and serving.

Oysters served on the half shell, whether raw or cooked, are always served in the deeper cup. "Shucking" (opening) raw oysters takes a bit of practice and is extra work for those recipes where you will be cooking the oysters. If you plan to grill, broil, or bake the oysters on the half shell, par-cooking them (steaming or baking for 2 or 3 minutes) prior to shucking will make the procedure much easier.

Conventional wisdom suggests cooking oysters for a maximum of 7 minutes, but I find that anything less than 10 minutes simply feels gelatinous in my mouth. Like many sensual pleasures, oysters are an acquired taste and the associated mouth-feel is a matter of personal preference; some people like them raw, others like them barely cooked. Personally, I like them hard as marbles, which scores me no points whatsoever with the food police (most of whom side with The Opposition in the great crunchy versus slimy debate). While it's true that there are solid biochemical principles governing the chemistry of flavour, that doesn't mean you should jump on the foodie bandwagon just because it's there: taste one after a total cooking time of 7 minutes to see what *you* think.

About Mussels
Mussels are the most forgiving of the bivalves: they will tolerate some overcooking, are generally free of sand, and are the easiest to shell. Mussels attach themselves to any available hard surface, including rocks, boats, and marine pilings, using tough fibres collectively called the "beard." These fibres are attached to the animals' insides, not just the shells' exterior, and should not be pulled off until just prior to cooking. Most commercially available mussels are sold beardless, so you only have to worry about beards if you have harvested them yourself.

About Clams
Unlike other bivalves, clams need a little extra attention prior to cooking. Most commercially available oysters and mussels are cultivated in a controlled environment where they are permanently attached to a hard (clean) surface. However, clams are primarily harvested wild from the ocean floor. They burrow into sand, anywhere from 4 inches to 3 feet (10 cm to 91 cm) deep, siphoning water as a means of propulsion and sucking in almost as much sand as seawater when they move.

To clean clams, some cooks suggest soaking them in water mixed with a little cornmeal (the clam will spit out the dirt as it feeds on the cornmeal) but, personally, I think that half-digested cornmeal is almost as unappealing as undigested sand. A tastier alternative is to soak clams for two hours in salted water, made by adding ⅓ cup (80 mL) of salt per gallon (4 litres) of water.

Hand-harvested Pacific clams are a best choice in terms of environmental impact and sustainability.

Bacon-wrapped Oysters

Bacon is a popular wrapping for a variety of foods ranging from beef tenderloin to scallops but the contrast between fresh briny oysters and crispy bacon is particularly enticing. Par-cooking the oysters makes them much easier to wrap, and par-cooking the bacon not only renders the fat, but also narrows the disparate cooking times between the two foods.

1. In a large frying pan, on medium-low heat, par-cook the bacon until most of the fat has rendered (do not allow it to crisp). Drain on paper towels until cool enough to handle.
2. Drain the oysters in a colander. Cut any large ones in half and season liberally with freshly ground pepper.
3. In a medium, non-stick frying pan, melt the butter on medium heat and par-cook the oysters until they firm up slightly, about 3 minutes, to make it easier for wrapping the bacon (otherwise they tend to implode during staking).
4. Cut the par-cooked bacon slices in half and wrap one piece of bacon around each oyster, overlapping the edges slightly. Stake each oyster with a cocktail stick and bracket the oyster on both sides with a chunk of red onion.
5. Preheat the broiler to high and broil the oysters close to the heat until the bacon is crisp and the oyster is cooked through, about 2 minutes (or more, according to taste). Serve immediately with Cocktail Sauce (p. 118).

12 oz (355 mL) freshly shucked oysters
1 tsp (5 mL) unsalted butter
8 slices thick-cut bacon
freshly ground pepper, to taste
1 small red onion, quartered
16 cocktail sticks, soaked in water for at least 15 minutes
Serves 4 as a starter.

Beer Suggestion: Guinness stout

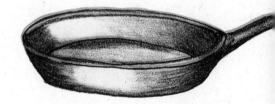

Oyster Shooters

This isn't really a recipe for raw oysters on the half shell so much as instructions on how to choke them down. To the self-described oyster connoisseur, I have no doubt revealed myself as both a heretic and a philistine, but I personally don't eat these; I find the experience entirely too reminiscent of a bad cold. I'm told actually chewing them greatly enhances the experience, but this is one experiment I can't bring myself to replicate. Notwithstanding my own personal prejudice, however, the wild popularity of this dish guarantees it a place in any West Coast cookbook.

1. Shuck the oysters (see p. 35), and arrange them on a platter of crushed ice. Serve immediately with lemon wedges and Tabasco sauce.
2. To eat, tip the oyster into your mouth and slurp both the oyster and any liquid that has collected in the bottom shell (called the "liquor") into your mouth. Chew before swallowing (bet you've never seen that in a recipe before!). Try sincerely not to gag.

8 raw oysters

1 oyster knife

lemon wedges

Tabasco sauce

Serves 4 as an appetizer.

Drink Recommendations: Mouthwash? *Okay, okay* . . . ice cold vodka, champagne or Guinness stout. Lots of it.

How to Shuck an Oyster

1. Safety is paramount. I am not generally a "gadget" person, but I cannot stress this enough: do not ad lib when it comes to shucking oysters. Use a sturdy oyster knife. Do not use a kitchen knife, or a screwdriver, or a hammer—or any of the other miscellaneous implements floating around in your kitchen junk drawer.

2. Wear sturdy gloves (rubber gardening gloves work well). This will prevent the oyster from slipping, and (possibly) a trip to the ER.

3. **Do not allow children to shuck oysters.**

4. Hold the oyster, cup side down, in your non-dominant hand, with the hinge facing towards you. Holding the oyster knife in your dominant hand, insert the knife tip between the shells at the hinge and twist the knife to pry the shells about half an inch (1 cm) apart. Run the blade counter-clockwise along the upper shell, severing the top adductor muscle.

5. The oyster shells will separate slightly, but do not yank them apart at this point; if the oyster is stuck to the upper shell, you will tear the meat. Instead, use your oyster knife to gently scrape the oyster from the topshell as you gently pull the shells apart.

6. Look inside the topshell, noting the remaining "scar" where the severed adductor muscle was attached to the shell. Find the corresponding place on the lower shell—this is where the oyster is still attached to the bottom shell. Use your to knife sever this muscle and free the oyster. Examine the oyster to ensure that no bits of shell have stuck to the meat.

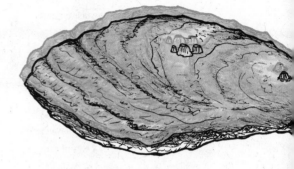

West Coast Clambake

Traditional New England clambakes are complicated affairs involving huge gobs of time, elaborate firepits on the beach, acres of wet canvas, large stones, buckets of freshly harvested seaweed, and (potentially) an impromptu visit from your friendly neighbourhood fire department. It is much easier to replicate a clambake at home using your barbecue.

24 small live clams

⅓ cup (80 mL) salt, dissolved in 1 gallon (4 litres) cold water

5 heavy-duty (disposable) aluminum foil loaf pans

1 lb (500 g) fresh seaweed OR ¾ lb (375 g) untreated hardwood chips, dampened with water

4 ears of corn

4 medium whole, unpeeled red potatoes

4 chicken thighs

1 Tbsp (15 mL) canola oil, for brushing

½ cup (125 mL) melted butter, divided

2 live Dungeness crabs

2 tsp (10 mL) sea salt

freshly ground pepper, to taste

Serves 4.

Beer Suggestion: Cold lager

1. Scrub the clam shells and soak them in the salted water for 2 hours.
2. Preheat the barbecue to medium (350°F [180°C]). Use a small screwdriver or a nail to poke multiple holes in the bottoms of all the loaf pans to allow any liquid to drain so your food will grill and smoke, rather than poach. Place the seaweed or damp (not soaked) hardwood chips in one loaf pan and set it directly on the barbecue grill, off to one side.
3. To partially shuck the corn, peel back the husks and remove all the silk before pulling the outer husks back over the kernels. Add one ear of corn and one potato to each remaining loaf pan, and set all four directly onto the grill at the back of the barbecue.
4. Brush the chicken thighs with the canola oil and grill, skin side down, directly on the grill for 5 minutes to sear the skin. Remove the chicken from the grill and add one piece to each loaf pan. Drizzle 2 tablespoons (30 mL) of the melted butter into each tin. If using wood chips, check to see they have not dried out; dampen with water if necessary. Close the barbecue lid, reduce the heat to medium-low, and grill the tins for 15 minutes.
5. While the chicken cooks, kill and clean the crab (p. 7), discarding the topshells. Separate the legs and claws, leaving the body meat attached to the top of each leg.

6. When the chicken reaches about 165°F (70°C) on an instant-read meat thermometer (after about 20 minutes of cooking), add 1 crab claw and 3 legs to each pan and drizzle in the remaining melted butter. Close the barbecue, increase the temperature to high (500°F [260°C]), and cook for 5 minutes.

7. Drain and rinse the clams. Add 6 clams to each pan, close the barbecue, and cook until the crab shells turn bright red and the meat is white and opaque, and all the clams are open, about 5 minutes (discard any clams that remain closed).

8. Season with salt and pepper and serve in the foil tins, with a plate underneath to catch the drips.

"Smoking" on the Barbecue

Real clambakes rely on fresh, hot seaweed to add a briny, smoky flavour to a hotchpotch of food, so the list of ingredients for your average clambake recipe tends to be somewhat sparse in the seasoning department. If you are lucky enough to get your hands on fresh seaweed, soak it in seawater for 45 minutes prior to cooking. Fresh seaweed is fairly hard to source if you don't live on the coast, in which case, substitute hardwood smoking chips that have been briefly dipped in salted water (do not soak the chips for an extended period of time, or you'll get more steam than smoke).

Oysters Rarebit

Traditional Welsh rarebit is cheese sauce on toast, while oysters rarebit is usually shucked oysters suspended in cheese sauce served on toast. I love both the sauce and the oysters but, not being partial to soggy bread, I prefer to eliminate the middleman and spoon the sauce directly over oysters on the half shell and serve them with a loaf of fresh, crusty bread on the side.

Oysters

24 small live oysters, in the shell

3 Tbsp (45 mL) melted butter

crumpled aluminum foil,
for keeping oysters upright

Sauce

2 Tbsp (30 mL) unsalted butter

2 Tbsp (30 mL) flour

¼ tsp (1 mL) mustard powder

½ tsp (2 mL) salt

freshly ground pepper, to taste

reserved oyster liquor, topped up with enough
whipping cream to make 1 cup (250 mL)

½ cup (125 mL) London Porter
or another dark beer

1 tsp (5 mL) Worcestershire sauce

½ cup (125 mL) grated Gruyère cheese

Serves 4.

Wine Suggestion: Unoaked chardonnay

1. Scrub the oysters and steam or bake them for 2 or 3 minutes prior to shucking. Par-cooking them will make them much easier to open. Shuck the oysters (p. 34) and pour the oyster liquor into a measuring cup. Return the oyster meat to the bottom shells.
2. Crumple a large sheet of aluminum foil onto a baking sheet, and arrange the oysters on the half-shell in the crevices to keep them stable. Brush each oyster with melted butter.
3. Preheat the broiler to high.
4. In a medium saucepan, melt the butter on medium heat, and then whisk in the flour, mustard powder, salt, and pepper. Cook for about 3 minutes, but do not allow the mixture to brown. Gradually whisk in the cream/oyster liquor mixture, the beer, and the Worcestershire sauce.
5. Place the oysters under the grill and broil them for 4 minutes.
6. Sprinkle the grated cheese over the sauce and whisk until it is smooth and the cheese is melted, about 1 to 2 minutes. Remove the oysters from the oven and spoon the sauce directly into the open shells, covering the oyster meat. Return to the broiler and grill for another 3 minutes until browned and bubbling.

Cliffy's Notes

Pacific oysters taste best when harvested between late November and late April. Oysters reproduce during the warm summer months, and their anatomical changes (including gender reversal from male to female, or female to male) reduce their flavour significantly during this time. After spawning, oysters are considerably less meaty—almost watery—and they need a couple of months to fatten up again. They will gain weight by producing glycogen, a starch that later converts into the simple sugar glucose, which gives shellfish its sweet taste. Of course, you can harvest oysters in the summer (safely disregarding that old adage about never harvesting oysters during months without an "R") but they will be plumper and sweeter from late fall until late spring.

Pan-fried Oysters with Champagne Sauce

Unless you're actually serving oysters on the half shell, buy them fresh in pint tubs and save the trouble of shucking them yourself. When buying oysters by the tub, double-check that the liquid in the container is clear and that the oysters themselves are plump and creamy looking. Freshly shucked, pre-packaged oysters have a fridge life of about 3 days.

Champagne Sauce

5 Tbsp (75 mL) unsalted butter, divided
1 Tbsp (15 mL) flour
1 cup (250 mL) Fish Stock (p. 160) (or substitute chicken stock)
1 egg yolk
1 Tbsp (30 mL) whipping cream
⅛ tsp (0.5 mL) nutmeg
1 cup (250 mL) champagne
1 shallot, minced

Serves 4.

Wine Suggestion: Champagne

Champagne Sauce

1. In a small saucepan, melt 1 tablespoon (15 mL) of the butter on medium heat. Whisk in the flour and cook the mixture until the flour starts to brown, about 2 to 3 minutes.
2. Whisk in the stock and bring it to a high simmer. Cook until the liquid reduces by half. Remove the mixture from the heat and allow it to cool long enough for the temperature to drop by about 20°F (11°C), about 2 minutes (the temperature must be under 180°F (82°C) when you add the egg or the yolk will scramble; set the pan in a bowl of ice water if you're in a hurry, and check the temperature with a candy thermometer if you're in a panic).
3. In a small bowl, beat the egg yolk with the cream and nutmeg. When the stock is cooled, whisk the egg mixture into the stock..
4. In a second saucepan, simmer the champagne with the shallot on medium heat until the liquid is reduced to ¼ cup (60 mL), about 5 minutes. Take the mixture off the heat and add the remaining butter, 1 tablespoon (15 mL) at a time, whisking between each addition.
5. Add the champagne reduction to the stock and stir to combine.

Oysters

1. In a large frying pan on medium heat, heat the water to a simmer and poach the oysters until just firm, about 5 minutes. Pat dry with paper towels and let cool, about 15 minutes.
2. On a large plate, stir together the flour, salt, pepper, and red pepper flakes. On a second plate, spread out the breadcrumbs.
3. Dredge the oysters one at a time in the flour, patting each one gently between your palms to remove the excess. Dip each floured oyster in the egg, and then roll it in the breadcrumbs, coating it completely. Set each breaded oyster on a wire rack and allow to dry for at least 15 minutes.
4. In a large, well-seasoned frying pan, heat the olive oil on high until very hot but not smoking. Pan-fry the oysters 4 or 5 at a time (depending on the size of your pan), turning them once, until the breading is golden brown and oysters reach your desired firmness, about 1 to 3 minutes per side.
5. Drain oysters briefly on paper towels and serve piping hot with Champagne Sauce on the side.

Cliffy's Notes

While Pacific Oysters can grow to nearly a foot (30 cm) in length, they are tastiest when their total shell length is about 2 to 3 inches (5 to 8 cm). Larger oysters are not necessarily tough, but their digestive mechanisms become more apparent, which makes them considerably less appetizing.

Oysters

½ cup (125 mL) water

1 pint (500 mL) small, freshly shucked oysters

1 cup (250 mL) flour

1 tsp (5 mL) salt

freshly ground pepper, to taste

½ tsp (2 mL) red pepper flakes

2 eggs, lightly beaten and
in a wide shallow bowl

2 cups (500 mL) Panko breadcrumbs

¼ cup (60 mL) canola oil, for frying

Thai Curried Mussels

Homemade Thai curry pastes are easy to make; the tricky part is sourcing the ingredients. The distinctive taste of these pastes relies partly on galangal, a root from the ginger family, which is available fresh or bottled in brine in Asian grocery stores If you can't find it, substitute regular ginger—or simply buy a good-quality commercially prepared Thai curry paste from your local grocery store.

Thai Green Curry Paste

Thai Green Curry Paste

6 fresh jalapeno peppers (or other fresh green chilis), chopped

1 medium onion, chopped

2 garlic cloves, chopped

1 tsp (15 mL) chopped fresh or brined galangal

¼ cup (60 mL) chopped fresh cilantro

1 Tbsp (15 mL) minced fresh lemon grass

1 tsp (5 mL) ground coriander

½ tsp (2 mL) ground cumin

1 tsp (5 mL) kaffir lime zest

1 tsp (5 mL) dried shrimp paste

½ tsp (2 mL) black pepper

¼ cup (60 mL) canola oil

Makes about 1½ cups (375 mL).

1. Place all ingredients, except the oil, in a blender and pulse to combine. Gradually add the oil and process until you get a smooth paste. This paste will keep in a glass jar in the fridge for up to 4 months.

Thai Red Curry Paste

1. Soak the dried chilis in hot water for 10 minutes. Discard the water, and then place all the ingredients, except the oil, in a blender and pulse to combine. Gradually add the oil and process until you get a smooth paste. This paste will keep in a glass jar in the fridge for up to 4 months.

Mussels

1. Rinse the mussels under cold running water (if using wild mussels, also scrub them with a stiff brush and pull off their beards). Discard any mussels that do not close when you handle them.
2. In a pan large enough to hold all the mussels (preferably in a single layer), whisk the curry paste into the coconut milk. On medium-high heat, bring the liquid to a high simmer. Add the mussels, stirring to coat them, and bring the mixture back up to a simmer.
3. Reduce the heat to medium, cover, and poach until all the mussels are open, about 4 or 5 minutes (discard any mussels that remain closed). Stir again to fully coat the mussels with the curried coconut milk and serve immediately.

Thai Red Curry Paste

6 dried red chili peppers

1 medium onion, chopped

2 garlic cloves, chopped

1 Tbsp (15 mL) chopped fresh or brined galangal

2 Tbsp (30 mL) chopped fresh cilantro

1 Tbsp (15 mL) minced fresh lemon grass

2 tsp (10 mL) ground coriander

1 tsp (5 mL) ground cumin

1 tsp (5 mL) ground tumeric

1 tsp (5 mL) paprika

2 tsp (10 mL) dried shrimp paste

½ tsp (2 mL) salt

½ tsp (2 mL) black pepper

¼ tsp (60 mL) canola oil

Makes about 1½ cups (375 mL).

Mussels

2 lb (1 kg) live mussels, in the shell

2 Tbsp Thai Green or Red Curry Paste (p. 42–43)

1 12-oz (355 mL) can coconut milk

Serves 4 as a starter.

Wine Suggestion: Pinot Gris

Grilled Oysters with Anchovy Pesto

Traditional pesto is a basil-leaf purée bound with olive oil and flavoured with Parmesan cheese and pine nuts, but you can vary the flavour by substituting other leaves, nuts, or cheeses—or by adding non-traditional ingredients such as anchovies.

Anchovy Pesto

Anchovy Pesto

¼ cup (60 mL) pine nuts
2 anchovy fillets, drained
2 cups (500 mL) fresh basil leaves
1 garlic clove, roughly chopped
½ cup (125 mL) freshly grated Romano cheese
½ cup (125 mL) extra virgin olive oil
Makes about 1 cups (250 mL).

1. Preheat the oven to 350°F (180°C). Spread the pine nuts on an ungreased baking sheet and roast for 10 minutes, stirring occasionally. Remove from the oven and allow to cool.
2. In a food processor, process the anchovies, basil, and garlic. Add the cheese and pulse to combine. Gradually add the oil, pulsing and holding for a few seconds between each addition. Transfer the pesto to a glass jar and drizzle a little olive oil on the top to seal the purée. While it is best fresh, it will keep in the fridge for a day or two (basil leaves oxidize quickly and the pesto will start to darken within 24 hours), or a couple of weeks in the freezer.

Oysters

Oysters

16 small live oysters, in the shell
Serves 4 as a starter.

Wine Suggestion: Sauvignon Blanc

1. Preheat the barbecue to medium (350°F [180°C]), clean and oil the grill, and then increase the heat to high (500°F [260°C]).
2. Scrub the oysters under running water and place them directly on the grill for 5 minutes. The par-cooked oysters should be easy to open at this point. Use an oven mitt to hold the oyster while you pop off the topshell with your oyster knife.
3. Spoon 1 tablespoon (15 mL) of Anchovy Pesto into each oyster shell, covering the meat. Grill for another 1 to 5 minutes, according to taste, and serve piping hot.

Mussels Poached in Wine

One of the reasons I love visiting my parents at the north end of Vancouver Island is their sailboat, which is anchored about 200 metres from their back door. As much as I love "stomping"—sailing in a gale force wind—the highlight of "The Boat" is rowing out to harvest the wild mussels that attach themselves to the buoy rope below the waterline. (I admit my joy is tempered by the long, disgustingly flabby sea worms one inevitably grabs while detaching mussels from the rope.)

1. Scrub the mussels with a brush under running water and set aside. (If using wild mussels, also pull off the beards.)
2. In a frying pan large enough to cook all the mussels in a single layer, melt the butter on medium heat and sauté the garlic, onion, bay leaf, and pepper until the onion is transparent, about 3 minutes (do not brown).
3. Add the white wine and bring to a boil. Reduce the heat to low and simmer for 5 minutes.
4. Turn the heat back up to high and add the mussels. Cover and poach until all the mussels are open, about 3 or 4 minutes. Serve immediately, discarding any mussels that remain closed.

4 lb (1.8 kg) live mussels, in the shell

¼ cup (60 mL) butter

4 garlic cloves, squashed with the flat side of a large chef's knife

1 small yellow onion, sliced

1 bay leaf

freshly ground pepper, to taste

1 cup (250 mL) dry white wine

Serves 8 as a starter.

Wine Suggestion: Muscadet

Steamed Clams in Salsa Negra

For an informal gathering, stir the clams into the salsa and serve as a dip with tortilla chips. For more of a presentation piece, spoon a bit of salsa into each clam shell, and then top with a steamed clam and a tiny sprig of cilantro.

Clams

1 gallon (4 L) cold water

⅓ cup (80 mL) salt

2 lb (1 kg) small live clams, in the shell

Salsa Negra

3 Tbsp (45 mL) dark brown sugar

1 tsp (5 mL) molasses

¼ cup (60 mL) canola oil

2 oz (60 g) dried chipotle chilies

2 garlic cloves, minced

½ tsp (2 mL) salt

Serves 8 as buffet finger food, or 4 as a starter.

Clams

1. Dissolve the salt in the water and soak the clams for 2 hours so they spit out any sand. Drain and rinse the clams, discarding any that do not close when you handle them.
2. In a covered pan large enough to hold them all, steam the clams in their own juices on medium-high heat until they all open. Discard any that remain closed, and cool the rest to room temperature.
3. When the clams are cool enough to handle, after about 5 minutes, remove the meat, reserving the shells for presentation.

Salsa Negra

1. In a small saucepan on medium-high heat, simmer ⅔ cup (160 mL) water with the sugar and molasses.
2. In a small frying pan, heat the oil on high heat until very hot but not smoking. Add the chilies and cook until they puff up, about 2 minutes. Using a slotted spoon, remove the chilies from the pan and drain on paper towels.
3. Add the garlic to the oil, reduce the heat to medium-low, and sauté until fragrant.

4. Transfer the sugar water, chilies, and garlic (but not the oil) to a blender and process until smooth (soak up the remaining oil with paper towels and discard it).

5. Return the purée to the saucepan. Add the salt and simmer sauce on medium-low until the mixture is thick and syrupy, about 20 minutes.

Salsa

1. Blanch and peel the tomatoes (see p. 100). Remove and discard the seeds and dice the pulp. In a medium mixing bowl, combine the tomatoes with the rest of the Salsa ingredients.

2. Spoon the Salsa equally into all the bottom clamshells, top with a steamed clam and a sprig of cilantro, and serve.

Salsa

3 Roma tomatoes

1 large garlic clove, minced

2 poblano chilies, seeded and diced

2 jalapeno chilies, seeded and diced

1 small white onion, diced

freshly squeezed juice from 2 limes

2 Tbsp (30 mL) chopped fresh cilantro

½ tsp (2 mL) salt

1 Tbsp (15 mL) Salsa Negra (p. 46)

cilantro sprigs, coarsely chopped, for garnishing

West Coast Bouillabaisse with Rouille

"West Coast bouillabaisse" is, at best, a contradiction in terms, as only recipes that call for at least a half-dozen species of Mediterranean seafood can legitimately use the label *bouillabaisse*. The succulent cold-water fish and shellfish typically harvested off the BC coast, however, more than give the French version a run for its money. In keeping with the original recipe, this recipe calls for non-oily fish (which pretty much eliminates salmon), and is served with Rouille (p. 49) and crusty peasant bread.

1. In a deep cast-iron frying pan (or a dutch oven), heat the olive oil on medium and sauté the garlic, onion, bay leaves, fennel, thyme, cayenne pepper, orange zest, saffron, salt and pepper until fragrant, about 3 minutes (do not brown). Stir in the tomatoes and cook until tomatoes are softened, about 10 minutes.
2. Add the halibut chunks and enough boiling water to cover the fish (bouillabaisse is the one exception to the "low simmer" poaching rule, and the particular flavour of this stew is due, in part, to the higher cooking temperature). Add the prawns and turn the heat up to high, boiling for 2 minutes before adding the cod.
3. Add the mussels, cover, and reduce the heat to low. Simmer until the mussels are all fully open, about 5 minutes. Discard any mussels that remain closed.
4. Slice the peasant bread and spread 4 slices with Rouille. Place each slice in a soup bowl and ladle the hot broth over the bread. Scoop the seafood out of the broth and arrange it on a large, warmed serving platter. Serve immediately with additional Rouille on the side.

Bouillabaisse

¼ cup (60 mL) olive oil

3 garlic cloves, minced

1 medium onion, chopped

2 bay leaves

1 sprig fresh fennel, chopped

1 sprig fresh thyme, chopped

1 tsp (5 mL) cayenne pepper

zest from one small orange

1 pinch saffron

1 tsp (5 mL) sea salt

freshly ground pepper, to taste

2 medium fresh tomatoes, blanched, peeled, and chopped (or substitute 1 14-oz (398 mL) can high-quality whole Italian tomatoes, drained and chopped)

boiling water, to cover the seafood

¾ lb (375 g) boneless, skinless halibut fillet, rinsed and patted dry with paper towels, cut into chunks

1 lb (500 g) large raw prawns, shell on

¾ lb (375 g) boneless, skinless cod fillet, rinsed and patted dry with paper towels, cut into chunks

1 lb (500 g) live mussels, in the shell

4 slices crusty peasant bread

1 recipe Rouille (p. 49)

Serves 4.

Rouille

Rouille is a hot and spicy mayonnaise-style sauce that makes a delicious garnish for seafood soups and stews. You need a starchy potato for this recipe, not a "new" one.

1. Broil the bell pepper in the oven close to the top element until it starts to blacken, and then turn it so the skin bubbles and browns on all sides. Place the pepper in a small bowl and cover it with plastic wrap until it's cool (this is the roasting equivalent of blanching). Once cool, the pepper will slide right out of its skin. Chop it into chunks and add it to your food processor bowl with the egg yolks, garlic, and chili pepper. Blend until smooth.

2. Add the cooked potato, saffron, cayenne, salt, and pepper, then purée until smooth. With the processor running, add the oil, in a very slow stream, and process until the sauce is thick. Transfer to a small serving bowl, and serve at the table, for adding to the bouillabaisse.

Rouille

1 large red bell pepper

2 egg yolks

3 garlic cloves, minced

1 jalapeno chili pepper, seeded and chopped

1 large, cooked russet potato

1 pinch saffron

1 tsp (5 mL) cayenne pepper

½ tsp (2 mL) sea salt

freshly ground pepper, to taste

1 cup (250 mL) olive oil

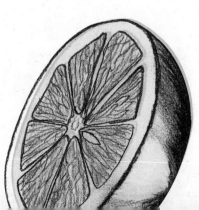

Oysters Rockefeller

The exact ingredients for this dish are the subject of much debate, as the original recipe, created in Louisiana more than a hundred years ago as a cheap alternative to *Escargots à la Bourguignonne* (snails in Burgundy sauce), has never been divulged. A licorice-flavoured liqueur is generally considered to be indispensable to Oysters Rockefeller, but other ingredients (bacon, hot sauce, and green food colouring, for starters), seem to come and go at the discretion of the cook.

⅓ cup (80 mL) unsalted butter

4 cups (1 litre) fresh spinach, stemmed and chopped

3 Tbsp (45 mL) minced onion

3 Tbsp (45 mL) minced parsley

2 Tbsp (30 mL) Pernod, or other licorice liqueur

½ tsp (2 mL) Tabasco sauce

½ tsp (2 mL) salt

freshly ground pepper, to taste

½ cup (125 mL) fine dry breadcrumbs

24 small live oysters, in the shell

crumpled aluminum foil, for baking

Serves 4 as an entrée, or 8 as a starter.

Wine Suggestion: Champagne

1. In a medium saucepan, melt the butter on medium heat and sauté the onion until transparent, about 3 minutes (do not brown). Add the spinach and parsley and cook until the greens are wilted, about 3 minutes more.

2. Stir in the Pernod, Tabasco, salt, and pepper; sauté for another 2 minutes. Remove the mixture from the heat, stir in the breadcrumbs, and set aside to cool.

3. Preheat the oven to 450°F (240°C). Scrub the oysters and steam or bake them for 2 to 3 minutes prior to shucking (p. 34)—parcooking them will make them much easier to open.

4. Loosely crumple a large sheet of aluminum foil and lay it flat on a baking sheet (the crevices in the foil will stabilize the oysters during cooking so they do not spill their sauce during cooking). Set the oysters in the foil, taking the time to make sure that they are level.

5. Divide the spinach mixture between the oysters, spreading it to the edge of each shell. Bake until the oysters are set, about 5 to 10 minutes, according to taste, and then switch the oven to broil. Move the oysters close to the heat for just long enough to brown the tops, about 1 to 2 minutes. Serve immediately.

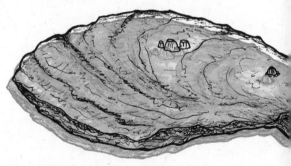

Grilled Clams
with Lemon Pepper Butter

A barbecue wok is a wok with holes that sits directly on the grill. Woks can be round or square and come in a variety of sizes. They are widely available through kitchen shops, barbecue dealers, and online (eBay has dozens of them). Using a wok is an easy way to grill small shellfish, as it prevents any meat falling out of the shells from landing in the coals (and it makes a nice change from the ubiquitous poaching recipes).

Lemon Pepper Butter

¼ cup (60 mL) unsalted butter
3 Tbsp (45 mL) Lemon Pepper (p. 53)
freshly squeezed juice from 2 lemons

Grilled Clams

2 lb (1 kg) small live clams, in the shell
1 gallon (4 L) cold water
⅓ cup (80 mL) salt
½ cup (125 mL) Lemon Pepper Butter (p. 53)
lemon wedges, for garnishing

Serves 4 as a starter, or 2 as an entrée.

Wine Suggestion: Sauvignon Blanc

Lemon Pepper Butter

1. In a small saucepan, melt the butter on low heat (or melt it in a glass measuring cup on low heat in the microwave). Stir in the Lemon Pepper and the lemon juice. Set aside while you grill the clams.

Grilled Clams

1. Scrub the clam shells. Dissolve the salt in the water and soak the clams for 2 hours so they spit out any sand. Drain and rinse the clams, discarding any that do not close when you handle them.
2. Preheat the barbecue to medium (350°F [180°C]), scrape the grill, and then increase the heat to high (500°F [260°C]). Rinse the clams well under running water and drain in a colander. If Lemon Butter has set, reheat briefly before adding it to the colander with the clams, stirring well to coat them on all sides.
3. Set the barbecue wok directly on the grill and pour in the clams. Stirring constantly, grill until all the shells are open, about 3 to 4 minutes; discard any clams that remain closed. Serve immediately with lemon wedges.

Lemon Pepper

1. Preheat the oven to 200°F (93°C). Wash and dry the lemons, and then use a potato peeler to zest the lemon, leaving the white pith on the fruit. Reserve the fruit for juicing later (wrapped in plastic, nude lemons will keep for a week in the refrigerator).

2. Spread the zest in a single layer on a cookie sheet and bake until it is dry and brittle, about 40 minutes. Remove from the oven and cool completely.

3. Crush the zest using a mortar and pestle and transfer to a clean glass jar with a screw-top lid. Add the salt and pepper, screw on the lid, and shake well to combine. Keep the Lemon Pepper in a cool, dark place for up to 4 weeks.

Lemon Pepper

zest from 6 whole organic lemons

3 Tbsp (45 mL) coarse kosher salt

1 Tbsp plus 1 tsp (20 mL) coarsely ground black pepper

Makes almost ⅓ cups (80 mL).

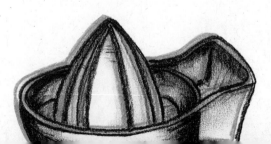

Spicy Mussel Linguine

The sauce will take about 20 minutes to thicken, so start with the sauce and allow it to simmer while you prepare the mussels and the pasta. When using canned tomatoes for a sauce, I find the texture is better if I buy high-quality whole Italian tomatoes and chop them coarsely myself rather than buying the crushed or diced ones.

3 Tbsp (45 mL) extra virgin olive oil
1 small onion, chopped
2 garlic cloves, minced
1 jalapeno pepper, seeded and minced
1 tsp (5 mL) red pepper flakes
½ tsp (2 mL) sea salt
freshly ground pepper, to taste
1 cup (250 mL) dry red wine, divided
1 28-oz (796 mL) can whole tomatoes
¼ cup (60 mL) tomato paste
4 lb (1.8 kg) fresh mussels, in the shell
¾ lb (375 g) dried linguine

Serves 4.

Wine Suggestion: Beaujolais

1. In a medium saucepan, sauté the onion in the olive oil on medium heat until it starts to brown, about 4 minutes. Add the garlic, jalapeno, pepper flakes, salt, and pepper and sauté for 1 minute more (do not brown the garlic).
2. Pour in ½ cup (125 mL) of the wine and simmer until the liquid is reduced by half, about 5 minutes. Roughly chop the tomatoes and add them to the saucepan. Stir in the tomato paste and simmer, uncovered, until the sauce thickens, about 20 minutes.
3.. Rinse the mussels and drain in a colander (if you are using wild mussels, pull off the beards and give them a good scrub with a stiff-bristled brush).
4. Bring a large pot of salted water to a rolling boil and cook the linguine until al dente, about 5 to 6 minutes, but taste-test to make sure. Drain the noodles but do not rinse them.

5. In a pan large enough to hold all the mussels, preferably in a single layer, bring the remaining wine to a boil, and then add the mussels. Cover and poach until all the mussels open, about 3 or 4 minutes. Discard any ones that remain closed.

6. Drain the mussels and discard the poaching liquid. Transfer to the saucepan containing the tomato sauce and toss to coat.

7. Divide the linguine between 4 warmed pasta bowls, top with the mussel sauce, and serve.

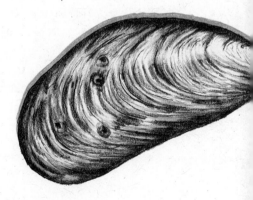

West Coast Clam Chowder

I first had this chowder many years ago in the American seaside town of Newport, Oregon, when my college roommate invited me down one American Thanksgiving to see the stunning coastline where she grew up. She fed me the most amazing chowder, loaded with baby butter clams and large Pacific spot prawns. I have replicated it many times, but nearly two decades later, Diane's "Newport" chowder remains the best I have ever eaten.

3 lb (1.5 kg) live baby butter clams, in the shell
1 gallon (4 L) cold water
⅓ cup (80 mL) salt
2 cups (500 mL) potatoes, peeled and diced
2 bay leaves
4 slices bacon, diced
1 large onion, minced
1 tsp (5 mL) Worcestershire sauce
2 garlic cloves, minced
2 Tbsp (30 mL) unsalted butter
2 Tbsp (30 mL) flour
1 lb (500 g) large raw prawns, shelled and de-veined
3 cups (750 mL) whole milk
1 cup (250 mL) whipping cream
freshly ground pepper, for garnishing

Serves 4.

Wine Suggestion: Chablis

1. Scrub the clam shells. Dissolve the salt in the water and soak the clams in a large pot or bucket for 2 hours so they spit out any sand. Drain and rinse the clams, discarding any that do not close when you handle them.
2. In a large saucepan, par-boil the potatoes, about 8 minutes; drain them and set aside.
3. In a medium skillet, cook the bacon and the onion on medium heat until the bacon is crisp, between 7 and 8 minutes.
4. Drain the clams and scrub them under cold running water. Place them in a large pot with the bay leaves, cover, and cook on high heat (the clams will poach in their own "nectar") until the shells open, discarding any that remain closed. Remove the clams and set aside, reserving the nectar in the pot.
5. Add the garlic and butter to the bacon skillet and sauté for 1 minute, and then whisk in the flour (do not allow the flour to brown).

6. Whisk in the Worcestershire sauce, and then gradually add the milk. Add the milk mixture to the reserved clam nectar and increase the heat to high until the milk starts simmering (do not allow it to boil). Add the par-boiled potatoes, reduce the heat to medium-low, cover, and simmer until they are cooked through.

7. Add the prawns, cover, and simmer until pink and opaque, about 3 to 4 minutes, depending on their size. Remove three-quarters of the clams from their shells and add the meat to the chowder. Add the whipping cream and stir until heated through.

8. Divide the remaining clams in their shell between 4 warmed soup bowls and ladle the chowder over the clams. Serve immediately with lots of freshly ground black pepper.

Oysters Grilled with Spicy Lemon Butter

This simple barbecue recipe is my favourite way to eat oysters. To prevent any lopsided shells from spilling their nectar into the barbecue, stabilize them using small stones or small balls of aluminum foil.

¼ cup (60 mL) melted unsalted butter

1 Tbsp (15 mL) Tabasco sauce

3 Tbsp (45 mL) freshly squeezed lemon juice

16 small live oysters, in the shell

1 Tbsp (15 mL) minced flat-leaf parsley, for garnishing

lemon wedges

Serves 4 as a starter.

Wine Suggestion: Chablis

1. In a small bowl, mix the melted butter with the Tabasco and the lemon juice; set aside.
2. Rinse the oysters under running water. Preheat the barbecue to medium (350°F [180°C]), clean and oil the grill, and then increase the heat to high (500°F [260°C]).
3. Place the oysters directly on the grill and par-cook for 3 or 4 minutes, so they are easier to open. Use your oyster knife to pry open the oysters, being careful not to spill the liquor from the bottom shell. Return the oysters to the barbecue and baste the oyster meat with the spicy lemon butter. Grill for another 2 minutes.
4. Divide the remaining spicy lemon butter between the oysters and sprinkle each one with a little parsley. Grill for another 1 to 5 minutes, according to taste. Serve piping hot with lemon wedges.

Salmon

About Salmon

Salmon really are the most amazing fish. They hatch in freshwater streams and tributaries, migrate hundreds of miles to the ocean, and then return several years later to the very same spot, in the very same river, to spawn. While the exact mechanism behind the homing system salmon use is not fully understood—though it appears to centre around chemical imprinting on the juvenile salmon's sense of smell—we do know that their extraordinary life cycle directly influences their culinary qualities. Salmon are biologically programmed to develop sufficient muscle tissue and fat stores to fuel their grueling upstream pre-spawning migration, which is why the fish is firm-fleshed and rich in fat.

As with all seafood, buy your salmon from a reputable fishmonger or a grocery store with a high turnover, clean glass-covered display cases, and buy it on the day you plan to eat it. If you must buy in advance, store salmon tightly wrapped in plastic in the coldest part of the refrigerator. Vacuum-packed, frozen salmon will keep for six months in the deep-freeze.

If you're shopping for a fresh, whole fish with the head intact, look for clear, bulging eyes, bright red (or pink) gills, and shiny scales. Don't be shy: you're going to pay top dollar for a whole salmon (or even a whole side), so ask questions. And ask to touch the fish. Salmon flesh should be resilient; if you leave a fingerprint in its side, it's beyond saving. If you're shopping for fillets or steaks, check to see that the fillets are moist and full, rather than thin and curling at the edges. Avoid salmon with a brownish tinge, as this is a sign of oil oxidation.

In Canada, much of the commercially available salmon is ocean-caged, farmed Atlantic salmon. Farmed salmon, however, is generally inferior in taste and texture to Pacific wild salmon and, after decades of trial and error, net-penning remains highly controversial in terms of its social, economic, and environmental impacts. It is undeniable that ocean-farmed salmon costs less than wild salmon, but in keeping with the "slow food" movement, we need to realize that high-quality food isn't expensive as much as mass-produced food is artificially cheap. The best choice you can make in terms of healthy oceans and sustainable fishing is wild Pacific salmon (all species) or self-contained (inland) American farmed salmon.

Culinary Importance of Rigor Mortis in Fish

The most sustainable salmon, of course, is the single hook-and-line fish that you've caught yourself. If you are lucky enough to harvest your own, immediately bleeding and gutting your catch will preserve its culinary integrity by eliminating the bacteria and digestive enzymes that hasten decomposition. Freshly cleaned fish should be iced, but further processing (filleting, steaking) should be delayed until after rigor mortis is complete.

Rigor mortis is the temporary stiffening of an animal carcass after death (which is why the slang term for a body at a crime scene is a "stiff"). All animals store energy in the form of glycogen; as the body metabolizes its supply, it creates lactic acid as a by-product (which is the same acid that makes your muscles stiff when you overdo it at the gym). When blood circulation ceases following death, lactic acid accumulates in the muscles and triggers chemical reactions that cause the proteins present to literally "lock" into position. Over time, the process reverses and the proteins will relax again but, in the case of fish, if you try to fillet prior to rigor mortis, there is no underlying structure to pull the muscle proteins back into their original positions. As a result, the shortened muscle proteins will make the flesh rubbery. However, a completely exhausted fish that has burned off *all* of its glycogen trying to stay out of the boat may not go into rigor mortis at all, which, from a gastronomic perspective, is not a good thing. Salmon that do not have the chance to complete rigor mortis tend to be gluey, while halibut tend to be white and chalky in texture. Which is one good reason not to overplay your fish.

Easy Pan-roasted Salmon Fillets

With pan-roasting, the initial frying in a very hot pan creates a wonderfully browned surface, while finishing the fish in a hot, "dry" oven cooks the fillets through without burning them. Pan-roasting is so easy, it frees you up to attend to other things, such as concocting the perfect sauce. Or having another glass of wine.

1. Set the oven to roast (not bake) and preheat it to 450°F (230°C). If using salmon with the skin left on, remove any scales using the back of a teaspoon. Rinse well, and pat dry with paper towels before seasoning both sides with salt and pepper.
2. For the crispiest fish, allow the fillets to "rest" in the fridge for 30 minutes, patting them dry a second time just prior to cooking. (Doing so removes any water drawn to the surface of the fish by the salt and prevents your fish from steaming.)
3. In an ovenproof cast-iron frying pan, heat the olive oil until it is very hot (it should shimmer, but not smoke). Add the fillets, skin side up (presentation side down) and sauté for 5 minutes.
4. Turn the fillets and place the entire pan on the middle rack in the preheated oven and cook for 4 minutes more. Remove fillets from pan and serve immediately.

4 5-oz (150 g) centre-cut, boneless salmon fillets (whether you leave the skin on or not is a matter of personal taste)
¼ cup (120 mL) olive oil
1 tsp (5 mL) sea salt
freshly ground pepper, to taste
Serves 4.

Wine Suggestion: Pinot Noir

Roasted Salmon with Seafood Stuffing

Placing a perfectly roasted salmon in the middle of your table during a dinner party makes a spectacular presentation, particularly if you leave the head and tail intact.

Seafood Stuffing

2 tbsp (30 mL) butter

¾ cup (180 mL) uncooked long-grain rice

2 garlic cloves, minced

¼ cup (60 mL) dry sherry

¾ cup (180 mL) water

2 green onions, minced

¼ cup (120 mL) minced fresh tarragon

1 cup (125 mL) cooked prawns, chopped

1 cup (125 mL) cooked crabmeat, chopped

½ tsp (2.5 mL) salt

freshly ground pepper, to taste

Salmon

1 whole 6- to 8-lb (3 or 4 kg) salmon, head and tail intact

1 tsp (5 mL) sea salt

1 tsp (5 mL) freshly ground pepper

1 Tbsp (15 mL) olive oil, for brushing

Serves 8 to 10, depending on the size of the fish.

Wine Suggestion: White Burgundy

Seafood Stuffing

1. In a medium saucepan, melt the butter on medium heat. Stir in the rice, cooking until it turns translucent, about 3 minutes. Add the garlic and stir-fry until fragrant, about 2 minutes (do not brown). Add the sherry and stir until all the liquid is absorbed. Add enough water to cover the rice (about ¾ cup) and bring it to a boil. Reduce heat to low and cook, uncovered, until all the liquid is fully absorbed, about 5 minutes. Remove from heat, cover, and set aside to cool.

2. When the rice has cooled to room temperature, stir in the green onion, tarragon, prawns, crabmeat, salt, and pepper; set aside until you are ready to stuff your fish (refrigerate if the interval exceeds half an hour).

3. This recipe yields about 4 cups (1 L) of stuffing so place any excess in a greased ramekin and bake in the oven next to the fish for 20 minutes.

Salmon

1. Scale and rinse the fish, and then pat it dry with paper towels. To estimate cooking time, measure the thickest portion of the fish (at the neck) and allow 10 minutes of cooking time per inch (2.5 cm) of thickness. Season the fish all over with salt and pepper, and let it rest in the fridge for 30 minutes.

2. Preheat the oven to 400°F (200°C). Line a large roasting pan with aluminum foil and coat lightly with olive oil. Pat the fish dry again with paper towels to remove any water brought to the surface by the salt. Brush the salmon with olive oil and set it in the roaster. Spoon the Seafood Stuffing into the fish cavity.

3. Brush a second sheet of foil with oil and cover the fish. Set the roaster on the oven's centre rack and bake for 20 minutes.

4. Remove the top layer of foil and baste the fish with the pan juice. Reduce the heat to 350°F (180°C) and return the fish to the oven. Continue to roast until you reach your estimated "done" time, or when an instant-read thermometer reads 125°F (52°C). Remove the fish from the oven, tent loosely with foil, and allow to rest in a warm place for 10 minutes prior to serving.

5. To serve a whole roasted fish, insert a sharp knife at a slight angle close to the head, and run it the length of the backbone, which will loosen the top fillet from the ribs and back. Cut the top fillet crosswise into serving-size pieces that can be easily removed from the backbone with a serving fork. Transfer the fish to a warmed platter and serve with the remaining stuffing.

Tandoori Salmon
with Mango Chutney

You can buy commercially prepared garam masala at many grocery stores, but it is easy and inexpensive to make if you have a spare coffee grinder and a few minutes of extra time (see p. 104). If you choose to make your own spice mix and want to mimic the bright red colour of commercially prepared tandoori pastes, add a few drops of red food colouring.

Tandoori Salmon

2 Tbsp (30 mL) butter

2 Tbsp (30 mL) peeled, minced fresh ginger

3 garlic cloves, minced

1 Tbsp (15 mL) garam masala (p. 104)

1 tsp (5 mL) chili powder

1 Tbsp (15 mL) minced fresh cilantro

½ tsp (2 mL) sea salt

2 or 3 drops red food colouring (optional)

4 5-oz (150 g) boneless, skinless salmon fillets

Serves 4.

Wine Suggestion: Pinot Noir

Tandoori Salmon

1. In a small saucepan, melt the butter on medium heat. Add the ginger and garlic, and sauté until fragrant, about 2 minutes (do not brown). Add the garam masala, chili powder, cilantro, salt, and food colouring (if using). Take the spice mixture off the heat and set it aside.

2. Preheat the broiler to high (500°F [260°C]). Rinse the salmon and dry well using paper towels before spreading spice paste evenly over both sides of fillets. Calculate cooking time based on 10 minutes total grilling time per inch (2.5 cm) of thickness. Arrange the fillets in a roasting pan and broil on top rack turning once, a little more than halfway through the total cooking time (the fish should just begin to flake in the centre).

3. Remove the salmon from the broiler and serve immediately, on warmed plates, with Naan Bread and Mango Chutney.

Naan Bread

1. In a non-stick frying pan, melt 2 tablespoons (30 mL) of butter on medium heat and briefly pan-fry each naan bread.

Mango Chutney

1. Wash and cut the mangoes. Remove the pits prior to peeling (peeled mangoes are slimy and the pits cling so you'll have a better grip if you halve and pit them with the skin on). Peel the pitted fruit and chop it into 1-inch (2.5 cm) cubes.

2. In a large saucepan, on high heat, combine the vinegar and sugar and bring this mixture to a boil. Immediately reduce the heat to low, add the mangoes and stir to coat.

3. Add the oil to a second, smaller saucepan, and fry the chili flakes and cinnamon on medium heat for 2 to 3 minutes. Add the red onion and ginger and cook until soft, about 4 minutes (do not brown).

4. Add the spiced onion mixture to the mangoes, and then add the raisins and dates. Cover and simmer on low heat for 1 hour. Take the mixture off the heat and allow it to cool completely. Transfer the chutney to a glass jar, cover, and refrigerate for up to two weeks.

Naan Bread

2 Tbsp (30 mL) butter

4 naan breads

Mango Chutney

3 lb (1.5 kg) ripe mangoes

2 cups (500 mL) white vinegar

1 cup (250 mL) brown sugar

1 Tbsp (15 mL) canola oil

2 tsp (10 mL) crushed red pepper flakes

1 tsp (5 mL) ground cinnamon

1 small red onion, diced

1 Tbsp (15 mL) minced fresh ginger

½ cup (125 mL) raisins

½ cup (125 mL) pitted dates, chopped

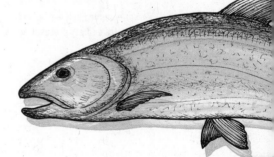

Cedar-planked Salmon

No West Coast seafood cookbook would be complete without a recipe for "planked" salmon—that grilling technique where a wooden board is first soaked in water, and then placed in a covered barbecue with the fish on top of it. The smoke generated by the charring wood gives the salmon a sublime smoky flavour and a firm but moist texture.

1 untreated cedar plank, large enough to comfortably hold the fish

2 to 3 cups (500 to 750 mL) boiling water

3 sprigs fresh thyme

3 garlic cloves, peeled and squashed

1 Tbsp (15 mL) whole peppercorns

2 Tbsp (30 mL) olive oil

2 Tbsp (30 mL) freshly squeezed lime juice

zest of 1 lime

2 Tbsp (30 mL) fresh thyme leaves, chopped

1 garlic clove, minced

1 whole side of salmon, about 2 lb (1 kg), skin left on

2 tsp (10 mL) freshly ground pepper

1 tsp (5 mL) sea salt

spray bottle filled with water (as a safety precaution)

Serves 4.

Wine Suggestion: Pinot Noir

1. Set the cedar plank in a large roasting pan. Add the garlic, thyme, and peppercorns, and then cover with enough boiling water to just cover the plank. Fill a small saucepan with water and set it on top of the plank to keep it submerged. Soak the plank for **at least** 1 hour, preferably 2 hours.
2. In a shallow, glass (non-reactive) baking pan, whisk together the olive oil, lime juice and zest, thyme, and garlic.
3. Scale and rinse the fish, and then pat dry with paper towels. Season the flesh side with salt and pepper, and then place skin side down in the marinade. Cover and refrigerate for 30 minutes, turning once halfway through.
4. Preheat the barbecue to medium (350°F [180°C]), and scrape the grill before increasing the heat to high (500°F [260°C]). Remove the plank from its soaking water and towel it dry; discard the marinade. Lightly oil the plank's top surface (do not oil the bottom) and set the fish skin side down on the oiled side (you will not be turning the fish at all during cooking).
5. Place the plank and fish directly on the grill and close the lid. Keep a close eye on the grill to ensure that the plank does not catch on fire (keep your spray bottle handy to put out any flare-ups), however, try to keep the lid closed as much as possible; trapping the cedar smoke inside the barbecue is what gives this recipe its delicious, smoky flavor.

6. Grill the fish for 10 minutes per inch (2.5 cm) of thickness, or until the salmon just starts to flake in the centre. Wearing flame-retardant grilling gloves, slide the plank off the barbecue and onto a baking sheet. Transfer the salmon to a serving platter (leave the skin on the plank if it sticks) and serve immediately.

Tips on Planking

If your local lumberyard sells untreated cedar or alder planks, it is most economical to buy them there. **Never use treated wood** to make planked salmon—the chemicals used to preserve lumber are highly toxic. If you can't find untreated wood at your local yard, appropriate planks are available at many department stores and kitchen shops, as well as online, however, they cost more.

Opinions vary on how long you should soak the plank. I always soak mine for a minimum of 2 hours, and I start with boiling water, as it seems to permeate the cedar a little better. Once the fish is on the grill, keep a spray bottle filled with water nearby to douse the flames just in case your plank does ignite.

Beer-battered Salmon

I first had salmon and chips in Nanaimo, BC, sold straight from a fishboat docked at the public wharf, and I quickly became a convert. Now, on those rare occasions when I haul out the deep fryer, I use boneless, skinless salmon fillets that I've coated in a crispy beer batter. They are particularly tasty served with coarsely ground sea salt and malt vinegar.

1. In a small bowl, beat the egg lightly with a fork and stir in the beer. In a large bowl, whisk together the flour, cornstarch, salt, pepper, and paprika. Gradually blend the wet ingredients into the dry ingredients (do not overmix). Cover and chill for at least 30 minutes.
2. Add the cooking oil to your deep fryer, paying close attention to the manufacturer's **maximum** (and minimum) fill lines. Preheat the oil to 375°F (190°C).
3. Rinse the salmon chunks and dry well using paper towels. Dust the salmon lightly with the flour to absorb any moisture remaining on the outside of the fish and shake off any excess.
4. Dip floured salmon pieces into the batter, draining off any excess, and lower no more than 4 pieces at a time carefully into the deep fryer. Close the lid and fry until batter turns golden brown, about 4 minutes. Drain on paper towels and serve immediately.

Batter

1 egg

¾ cup (175 mL) dark beer
(I use Fuller's London Porter)

¾ cup (175 mL) all-purpose flour

2 Tbsp (30 mL) cornstarch

1 tsp (5 mL) salt

1 tsp (5 mL) freshly ground pepper

1 tsp (5 mL) paprika

Fish

canola or safflower oil, for frying

1½ lb (750 g) skinless, boneless salmon fillets, cut into small rectangles, about 2 inches by 3 inches (5 cm by 8 cm)

½ cup (125mL) all-purpose flour, for dusting fillets

Serves 4.

Wine Suggestion: Riesling

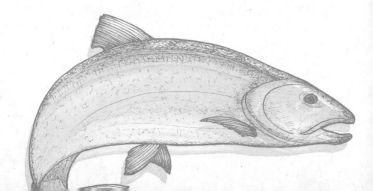

Perfect Chips, Every Time

For the crispest chips to accompany your fish, use high-starch russet potatoes and pre-fry them before cooking the fish. Peel them well in advance and cut them into uniform wedges (thick wedges will absorb less oil than skinny little matchstick potatoes). Soak them for half an hour in salted water to bring the starch to the surface, which helps give the chips a crispy "crust." Drain the potatoes and pat them dry with paper towels since wet potatoes introduce water into your deep fryer, which not only drops the temperature of the oil inside the fryer, but actually hastens its molecular deterioration.

To pre-cook, deep-fry the potatoes in small batches in your fryer at 350°F (180°C), until they turn a very pale gold, about 5 to 6 minutes, depending on the volume of your deep fryer. Drain the chips on paper towels and set them aside until cooled to room temperature. When it's time to serve the fish, fry them a second time at 375°F (190°C), until chips turn a deep golden brown, about 3 to 4 minutes.

Sesame-glazed Salmon Skewers

When buying salmon for skewers, choose a thick, centre-cut fillet that you can cut into fairly large chunks—a thin, flimsy fillet is far more likely to fall off the skewer. It is also easier to season fragile salmon cubes by soaking them in brine for 30 minutes, rather than trying to sprinkle them evenly on all sides with salt and pepper. Use metal skewers that are flat on one side to prevent the salmon from spinning when you turn it.

Brine

1. In a large, heat-proof mixing bowl that is large enough to hold all the fish and about 5 cups of water, add the salt, sugar, garlic, and pepper.
2. Pour in the boiling water and whisk until the solids are fully dissolved. Add the ice cubes to speed cooling, and then top up the mixture with the cold water. Cover and refrigerate for at least 30 minutes—the brine must be well chilled before you add the fish.

Glaze

1. In a small mixing bowl, whisk together the sesame oil, hoisin sauce, vinegar, and garlic; set aside.

Fish

1. In a small saucepan, heat the sesame seeds on medium heat until lightly toasted, about 5 minutes; set aside to cool.
2. Rinse the fillet and cut it into large cubes, about 1½ inches (4 cm) wide. Add the fish cubes to the cold brine, cover, and refrigerate for 1 hour.

Brine

1 cup (250 mL) coarse kosher salt

½ cup (125 L) white sugar

3 garlic cloves, peeled and squashed

1 tsp (5 mL) coarsely crushed black pepper

1 cup (250 mL) boiling water

8 ice cubes

3 cups (750 mL) cold water

Glaze

1 Tbsp (15 mL) dark sesame oil

3 Tbsp (45 mL) hoisin sauce

1 tsp (5 mL) white vinegar

2 garlic cloves, minced

Fish

2 Tbsp (30 mL) sesame seeds

2 lb (1 kg) boneless, skinless salmon fillet

3 Tbsp (45 mL) peanut oil

5-inch (12 cm) piece of fresh ginger root, sliced thinly

Serves 4.

Wine Suggestion: Gewürztraminer

3. Drain and rinse the fish cubes in a large colander, picking out any chunks of garlic and pepper. Discard the brine and pat the fish dry with paper towels. Preheat the barbecue to medium (350°F [180°C]), clean and oil the grill, and then increase the heat to high (500°F [260°C]).

4. In a large bowl, gently toss the cubes in the peanut oil, covering them on all sides. Thread the fish onto the skewers, alternating each cube with a slice of ginger.

5. Cook the skewers directly on the grill long enough for the fish to release easily from the grill, about 3 minutes. Turn the skewers and brush the tops liberally with the glaze. Grill until the salmon is just cooked, about 3 or 4 minutes longer. Transfer the skewers to a warmed serving platter, sprinkle with the toasted sesame seeds, and serve immediately.

Six Tips for Grilling Seafood

Start with a Perfectly Clean Grill

Every griller agrees on this point, but there is much dissension as to how it should be achieved. While soft-bristled, brass brushes are supposed to be less likely to break off on the grill than stiff steel ones, I have stayed away from wire brushes all together since reading about several small children who required emergency surgery after ingesting bristles along with their hamburgers. Instead, I use a pumice stone designed specifically for scraping grills. These stones can be purchased year-round at stores like Home Depot, but in a pinch you can also use a wad of crumpled aluminum foil. If you get a big chunk of burned-on barbecue sauce caught between the grates, scrape it off with a putty knife.

Get Organized

How many of us have dried out, ignited, or otherwise ruined a great piece of fish because we were trying to do too many things at once? Calculate your cooking times **before** you start to grill and plan the rest of your meal accordingly. For most seafood dishes, you will be grilling for only a few minutes. So don't put the fish on the barbecue and then go shuck the corn and make the salad; have everything else ready to go first.

Don't Leave Your Grill Unattended

This point is especially important when grilling seafood because it takes such a short time to cook: one ill-timed flare-up or an extra minute of cooking time can ruin your fish. This tip goes hand-in-hand with getting organized. To reduce steps between the kitchen and the barbecue, put all your grilling utensils and sauces on a tray or a cookie sheet, and take everything outside with you at once. Prepare your sides and accompaniments before you start to grill, set the table, uncork the wine . . . Whatever you have to do, do it before you put the fish on. That way you won't have any reason to leave your grill.

Calculate Cooking Times before You Start

Most fish fillets and steaks are cooked on medium-high for a short period of time. Whole fish take longer and so they should be grilled at a lower temperature to avoid drying out. Oily fish, such as salmon, are more forgiving of an extra minute or two on the grill, and firm fish fillets, such as halibut, work better for grilling than more fragile fish, such as sole. The chart on the next page summarizes total cooking times.

Seafood Grilling Times

Whole fish, measured at the neck	10 minutes per inch of thickness
Fillet or steak, ½ inch	5 minutes
Fillet or steak, 1 inch	8 to 10 minutes
Fillet or steak, 1½ inch	10 to 12 minutes
Prawns	3 to 4 minutes
Scallops	3 to 4 minutes
Mussels	4 to 5 minutes
Clams	7 to 8 minutes
Oysters	4 to 5 minutes
Crab	7 to 9 minutes

Turn Your Fish Once

And cook it slightly longer on the first side. This is important for three reasons. First, the longer you grill anything, the easier it comes off the grill and that extra minute on the first side will make the fish easier to turn. Second, the first side to be grilled is generally served facing up, and the clean-edged grill marks make for a pleasing presentation. Third, fish that is already warm will take less time to cook halfway than the cold fish that initially went on the grill; slightly reducing the cooking time for the second side reduces your chances of overcooking.

Leave the Skin on Fillets

Fully cooked fish is more fragile than raw fish, and if your fillet sticks or falls apart when you try to take it off the grill, slide a thin-lipped, metal spatula between the fillet and the skin and leave the skin behind on the grate.

Grilled Teriyaki Salmon with Shiitake Mushrooms

The sugar-based marinade used in this recipe increases the risk of your fish sticking to the barbecue, but this annoyance can be countered by oiling both the fish and the grill prior to cooking, as well as by choosing salmon fillets with the skin left on (instead of salmon steaks or skinless fillets). Start by grilling the flesh side first; it will take more than half the total recommended grilling time for the fish to release easily from the grill.

1. Squash the garlic cloves with the flat side of a chef's knife to pop them out of their skins, and then squash them a few more times to release the oil. Slice the ginger very thinly on the diagonal (do not mince the garlic or ginger since you will be picking it all off the fish later).

2. Add the garlic, ginger, sesame oil, soy sauce, sake, and sugar to a large, resealable plastic freezer bag. Zip it closed, and swish to blend all the marinade ingredients. Set aside.

3. Scale and rinse the salmon, and then pat dry using paper towels. Add the fish to the bag containing the marinade, reseal the bag, and turn to coat the fillets completely. Refrigerate the bagged fish for 30 minutes.

4. Once the fish has finished marinating, preheat the barbecue to medium (350°F [180°C]). Clean and oil the grill, and then increase the heat to high (500°F [260°C]). Drain the salmon on paper towels, picking off any remaining large pieces of ginger or garlic, and discard the marinade. Brush the fillets lightly with canola oil and then set the fish aside momentarily while you start the mushrooms.

Marinade

6 garlic cloves, peeled and squashed

4-inch (10 cm) piece of fresh ginger, sliced thinly on the diagonal

2 tsp (10 mL) sesame oil

¼ cup (60 mL) soy sauce

¼ cup (60 mL) sake

2 Tbsp (30 mL) light brown sugar

Salmon

4 5-oz (150 g) boneless salmon fillets, 1 inch (2.5 cm) thick, skin left on

1 Tbsp (15 mL) canola oil, for brushing

Mushrooms

1 lb (500 g) fresh shiitake mushrooms, stemmed and sliced

1 Tbsp (15 mL) canola oil

1 tsp (5 mL) pure sesame oil

Serves 4.

Wine Suggestion: Pinot Noir

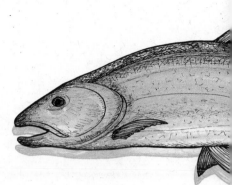

5. Preheat a medium frying pan on medium heat. Add the mushrooms and sauté for 1 to 2 minutes before adding the canola oil (preheating both the pan and the mushrooms prevents a few of the mushrooms from absorbing all of the oil). Sauté the mushrooms until they have released their liquid, about 4 minutes. Remove from heat and set aside briefly while you cook the fish.

6. Grill the salmon by placing the fillets directly on the grill, flesh side down. Flip the fillets once, when the salmon releases easily from the grill, about 7 minutes for 1-inch (2.5 cm) fillets.

7. Finish grilling the fish skin side down for 3 to 4 more minutes, and then slide a thin spatula between each fillet and its skin, leaving skin behind on the grill.

8. Bring the fillets back to the kitchen, and arrange the fillets on individual pre-warmed plates. Return the mushrooms to the heat and sauté briefly on high, about 1 minute. Stir in the sesame oil. Divide the mushrooms evenly over the salmon fillets and serve immediately.

Whole Chilled Salmon with Cucumber and Herbed Mayonnaise

Poaching Liquid

8 cups (2 L) water

1 large onion, chopped

1 large carrot, chopped

3 stalks celery, chopped

1 leek, chopped

2 bay leaves

2 sprigs fresh thyme

½ tsp (2 mL) coarse sea salt

1 tsp (5 mL) whole black peppercorns

2 cups (500 mL) dry white wine

Poached Salmon

6 to 8 lb (2.7 to 3.5 kg) whole salmon, head and tail intact

In this recipe, the dramatic presentation of a whole salmon is enhanced by a topping of herbed mayonnaise and overlapping cucumber slices, which combine to create the illusion of fish scales.

Poaching Liquid (or *court bouillon*, if you're French)

1. In a large stockpot, combine all the ingredients except the wine, and bring them to a boil. Reduce the heat to medium-low and simmer, uncovered, for 30 minutes.
2. Using a colander, strain the broth and discard the vegetables. Allow the liquid to cool completely (at least 30 minutes).
3. Stir in the wine, and then transfer the poaching liquid to a fish kettle (if you have one) or a turkey roaster.

Poached Salmon

1a. If using a turkey roaster, preheat the oven to 250°F (120°C). Scale and rinse the fish, leaving the head and tail intact. Measure the fish at its thickest point (the neck), and calculate the cooking time based on 12 minutes per inch of thickness. Add the cooled poaching liquid to the roaster and submerge the fish in the liquid, keeping it off the bottom of the pan with a wire rack. Transfer the roaster to the lowest rack in the oven and bake until an instant-read thermometer inserted into the backbone of the fish reads 130°F (55°C).

1b. If using a fish kettle, add the cooled poaching liquid to the pan and submerge the fish, keeping it off the bottom of the kettle with a wire rack. Set the kettle over two burners on the stovetop on medium-low heat. Bring the liquid to a low simmer and poach until an instant-read thermometer inserted into the backbone of the fish reads 130°F (55°C).

2. Remove the fish from its pan and allow it to cool for at least 1 hour while you make the Herbed Mayonnaise..

Herbed Mayonnaise

1. In a small mixing bowl, combine all the ingredients and mix well. Cover and refrigerate until the fish is ready to dress.

Dressed Salmon

1. Remove the skin by cutting through the skin all the way around the fish at the base of the head and again at the base of the tail. Then cut through the skin along the backbone from head to tail. Starting at the neck and working towards the tail, peel the skin off one side of the salmon; then turn the fish over and peel it off the other side. Gently scrape off the fat (brown meat).

2. Prior to dressing the fish, insert a sharp knife at a slight angle close to the head, and run it the length of the backbone to loosen the top fillet from the ribs and back. Cut the top fillet crosswise into serving-size pieces that can be easily removed from the backbone with a serving fork.

3. Cover the top fillet liberally with the Herbed Mayonnaise, and then, **starting at the tail,** layer overlapping cucumber slices on top to produce the illusion of fish scales. Cover loosely with foil and refrigerate until serving.

Herbed Mayonnaise

1 cup Blender Mayonnaise (p. 21)
2 Tbsp (30 mL) finely chopped fresh tarragon
1 Tbsp (15 mL) finely chopped fresh dill
1 Tbsp (15 mL) minced green onion
2 tsp (10 mL) fresh lime juice
½ tsp (2 mL) sea salt
freshly ground pepper, to taste

Dressed Salmon

1 whole Poached Salmon (p. 76), cooled
1 recipe Herbed Mayonnaise (p. 77)
1 long English cucumber,
peeled and sliced very thin
Serves 12 to 15.

Wine Suggestion: Sauvignon Blanc

Thai Curried Salmon and Mango Salad

While I would ordinarily add cold leftover seafood to salad, this hot salad calls for freshly grilled marinated salmon strips served over baby greens. It's a perfect combination of light and filling on a hot summer night when it's just too warm for a big meal.

Thai Curried Salmon

6 cloves garlic, peeled and squashed

4-inch (10 cm) piece fresh ginger, thinly sliced

3 Tbsp (45 mL) Green Thai Curry Paste (p. 42)

2 Tbsp (30 mL) canned coconut milk

1 Tbsp (15 mL) sesame oil

1 Tbsp (15 mL) soy sauce

2 lb (1 kg) large salmon fillet, pin bones removed but skin left on

Mango Salad

¼ cup (60 mL) lemon juice

¼ cup (60 mL) olive oil

zest from 1 lemon

8 cups (2 L) baby greens (spring mix)

1 sweet red pepper, seeded and thinly sliced

1 fresh mango, peeled and diced

¼ cup (60 mL) pine nuts

Serves 4.

Wine Suggestion: Sauvignon Blanc

1. Squash the garlic cloves with the flat side of a chef's knife to pop them out of their skins, and then squash them a few more times to release the oil. Slice the ginger very thinly on the diagonal.
2. Add the garlic, ginger, curry paste, coconut milk, sesame oil and soy sauce to a large, resealable plastic freezer bag. Zip it closed, and swish to blend all the marinade ingredients. Set aside.
3. Scale and rinse the salmon, and then pat dry using paper towels. Add the fish to the bag containing the marinade, reseal it, and turn to coat the fillet. Refrigerate for 30 minutes.
4. Once the fish has finished marinating, preheat the barbecue to medium (350°F [180°C]). Clean and oil the grill, and then increase the heat to high (500°F [260°C]). Drain the salmon on paper towels, picking off any remaining large pieces of ginger or garlic, and discard the marinade.
5. In a small glass (non-reactive) bowl, whisk together the lemon juice, olive oil, and lemon zest; set aside.
6. Wash and cut the mangoes. Remove the pits prior to peeling (peeled mangoes are slimy and the pits cling so you'll have a better grip if you halve and pit them with the skin on). Peel the pitted fruit and chop it into ½-inch (1 cm) cubes.

7. Divide the baby greens evenly between four large salad plates, and then top with the red pepper, mango, and pine nuts. Set aside while you grill the fish.

8. Set the salmon flesh side down directly on grill, calculating total cooking time at 10 minutes per inch of thickness. Grill the first side of a 1-inch (2.5 cm) fillet for about 7 minutes before using an extra wide metal spatula (or two smaller ones) to flip the fish to grill the other side turning (the extended time on the first side should make for easier turning).

9. Grill the fillet until the fish starts to flake in the middle, and then slide the metal spatula between the flesh and the skin and lift the whole fillet off the barbecue and onto a pre-warmed baking sheet, leaving the skin on the grill.

10. Use a very sharp carving knife to slice the salmon into 1-inch (2.5 cm) strips.

11. Drizzle salad dressing over each salad, topping with one quarter of the salmon. Serve immediately.

Smoked Salmon Benedict

Oh, the stress of serving eggs Benedict to guests! Relax. A basic understanding of the physics behind emulsions (along with lashings of champagne) goes a long way towards securing the success of this dish. Besides, these people are your friends, right? I mean, why else would you go to the trouble of making hollandaise from scratch? (See p. 82 for tips on emulsion sauces.)

Hollandaise Sauce

3 large egg yolks (plus 1 spare egg just in case), at room temperature

1 Tbsp plus 1 tsp (20 mL) lemon juice, at room temperature

1 Tbsp (15 mL) tepid water

½ cup (125 mL) unsalted butter

½ tsp (2 mL) salt

pinch cayenne pepper

Hollandaise Sauce

1. Mix the lemon juice and water in a small dish and set it aside. In a glass measuring cup, melt the butter on low in the microwave, about 1 to 2 minutes, depending on your microwave. The butter must be less than 180°F (82°C) when you add it to the egg or the yolks will scramble. The side of the measuring cup should feel warm to the touch, but not hot (use a candy thermometer if you're worried).

2. Prepare a double boiler: fill the bottom pan with enough water so that the top pan sits above the water, **not** in the water. Bring the water to a simmer, not a boil.

3. Add the egg yolks and lemon juice/water mixture to the upper pan and hand-whisk until the mixture gets frothy.

4. Add the warm butter to the eggs, 1 tablespoon (15 mL) at a time, hand-whisking constantly until the sauce thickens.

5. As soon as the sauce starts to thicken, remove the entire pan from the heat and whisk in the salt and cayenne pepper. Set the sauce aside while will you prepare the muffins but give it a stir every few minutes—it will keep for up to an hour.

Smoked Salmon Benedict

1. Split the English muffins into halves and arrange in single layer on a cookie sheet, ready for broiling. Flake the salmon into a small bowl and set aside while you poach the eggs.

2. Poach the eggs (see p. 82). As soon as the eggs are in the water, begin toasting the English muffins under the broiler. When toasted to your preference, remove from the oven and layer each muffin half with 1 oz (30 g) smoked salmon and toast again until the fish is warmed through, about 1 minute.

3. Remove the eggs from the poaching water and drain on paper towels. Remove the salmon-topped English muffins from the broiler, and top each half with 1 egg.

4. Briefly whisk the Hollandaise Sauce before spooning it liberally over each egg. Garnish with parsley sprigs and serve immediately.

Smoked Salmon Benedict

4 English muffins

8 oz (250 g) smoked salmon

8 eggs

1 recipe Hollandaise Sauce (p. 80)

8 sprigs parsley, for garnishing

Serves 4.

Wine Suggestion: Champagne

Hollandaise without Fear

Ordinarily, fat and water repel each other, as demonstrated by oil and vinegar salad dressing: when you shake the bottle, the water in the vinegar is broken into tiny droplets that are temporarily dispersed throughout the oil. Without an emulsifier the two incompatible liquids soon separate again. In the case of hollandaise sauce, melted butter is broken into tiny droplets that are suspended evenly throughout a small amount of water by vigorous whisking, and are held in place by the lipoproteins in the egg yolks.

While some recipes recommend that you add the lemon juice at the *end* of the recipe, adding the lemon juice (an acid) to the egg yolks at the *start* of the recipe raises the coagulation point of the yolks, making them less likely to curdle.

The sauce must be cooked at a temperature that is warm enough to keep the butter melted but not so warm that the eggs begin to scramble. You can most easily accomplish this balance by using a double boiler and keeping the water at a simmer, not a boil. If you add the butter too quickly, the emulsifiers in the egg yolks will not have time to coat the butter droplets, and the fat and water will separate. To prevent this separation from happening, add the melted butter 1 Tbsp (15 mL) at a time and whisk vigorously after each addition to fully incorporate the fat.

Curdled or separated sauce **can be salvaged**. Simply transfer the broken sauce to a bowl and strain out any solid pieces of cooked egg yolk. In the top pan of the double boiler, whisk an egg yolk with 1 Tbsp (15 mL) of water and 1 tsp (5 mL) of lemon juice. Set the top pan of the double boiler back over the simmering water and slowly whisk the broken sauce into the new egg-yolk mixture.

Perfect Poached Eggs
To avoid poached eggs that look like something you might spot through the Hubble Telescope, use only very fresh, "Grade A" eggs and bring them to room temperature prior to cooking.

Fill a large stockpot with 1 gallon (4 L) of water and add 3 Tbsp (45 mL) white vinegar and 1 Tbsp (15mL) salt. Bring the water to a low simmer. Crack the eggs, one at a time, into a shallow bowl and slide them, one at a time, into the stockpot. The eggs will sink to the bottom of the pot, and will float back to the top when they are nearly done. Give them one more minute, and then remove them using a slotted spoon. Drain them briefly on paper towels, trim off any "tentacles," and serve immediately.

Smoked Salmon Pâté

This smoked salmon pâté works well as buffet finger food or as a starter for a formal dinner. It pairs well with dark pumpernickel rounds.

1. Remove and discard the skin from the smoked salmon. Break up the fish with a fork, and then place it in a food processor and pulse until smooth.
2. In a non-stick frying pan, melt 2 tablespoons (30 mL) of the butter on medium, add the shallot, and sauté until transparent, about 2 minutes (do not brown). Remove the pan from the heat and set aside.
3. Add the lime juice, brandy, salt, pepper, and cooked shallot mixture to the salmon and pulse until smooth. Transfer the salmon paste from the food processor to a mixing bowl.
4. In a separate bowl, whip the cream until it forms soft peaks; fold it into the salmon mixture. Transfer the pâté to one large serving dish (or several small ramekins, depending on how you will be serving it) and smooth the top with an offset spatula.
5. Melt the remaining butter in the microwave and use it to brush the top of the pâté to prevent it from discolouring. Cover with plastic wrap and refrigerate until set, about 30 minutes. Garnish with parsley sprigs at serving time.

½ lb (250 g) smoked salmon
3 Tbsp (45 mL) unsalted butter, divided
2 shallots, minced
2 Tbsp (30 mL) freshly squeezed lime juice
1 Tbsp (15 mL) brandy
1 tsp (5 mL) sea salt
freshly ground pepper, to taste
⅓ cup (80 mL) whipping cream
parsley sprigs, for garnishing
Serves 8 as buffet finger food.

Salmon Wellington

Salmon Wellington is a common variation of classic beef Wellington, although the substitution of fish for the tenderloin prompts the omission of the *pâté de foie gras* commonly used to coat the beef. Considering that foie gras is produced by force-feeding geese until their livers enlarge by 6 to 10 times their normal size (in humans, don't we call that liver disease?), it is probably just as well.

Duxelles

1. In a frying pan, melt the butter on medium heat, add the onion, and sauté until soft but not brown, about 3 minutes. Add the mushrooms, tarragon, salt, and pepper. Cook until the mushrooms release their liquid and the mixture is fairly dry, about 10 minutes.
2. Add the white wine and simmer until the liquid is reduced by half. Reduce the heat to low and whisk in the cream. Remove the pan from the heat and allow the mixture to cool to room temperature, about 15 minutes.

Salmon Wellington

1. Preheat the oven to 400°F (200°C). Rinse the fish and pat it dry with paper towels (frozen fish must be thawed completely or the pastry will be a disaster). Season the fillets lightly on both sides with salt and pepper.
2. Roll out one sheet of puff pastry so it is about 2 inches (5 cm) wider and 2 inches (5 cm) longer than the fish fillets.
3. Place one fillet on the rolled pastry, spoon the Duxelles over it, and then top with a second fillet.

Duxelles

2 Tbsp (30 mL) butter

¼ cup (60 mL) minced onion

2 Tbsp (30 mL) minced fresh tarragon (or substitute 1 tsp [5 mL] dried)

3 cups (750 mL) minced fresh mushrooms

½ tsp (2 mL) sea salt

½ tsp (2 mL) freshly ground pepper

2 Tbsp (30 mL) dry white wine

¼ cup (120 mL) whipping cream

Salmon Wellington

2 centre-cut boneless, skinless salmon fillets, cut to equal size (about ½ lb [250 g] each)

½ tsp (2 mL) salt

freshly ground pepper, to taste

2 sheets frozen puff pastry, thawed

1 recipe Duxelles (p. 84)

1 egg, beaten

Serves 4.

Wine Suggestion: Riesling

4. Roll out second pastry sheet so it is 2 inches (5 cm) wider and 2 inches (5 cm) longer than first pastry sheet. Brush the edges of the bottom pastry with beaten egg before placing the second sheet of pastry over the stacked fish fillets. Seal the edges by pressing the entire perimeter firmly with a fork, and then trim off any ragged edges. Use the edge of a teaspoon to make an overlapping "fish scale" pattern on top of the pastry.

5. Brush the top of the pastry with beaten egg. Set on a lightly oiled baking sheet and bake until the pastry is golden and the fish is cooked through, about 30 to 35 minutes. Slice with a very sharp carving knife and serve immediately.

Duxelles?

Duxelles is a mushroom paste often used in conjunction with foie gras in traditional beef Wellington but it also pairs well with salmon. (However, there are countless other sauces and/or stuffings you can substitute if you don't like mushrooms.)

The flavour of the duxelles will vary according to which type of mushroom you choose to use, and wild mushrooms generally make a more savoury and intense paste than common white mushrooms. Using chanterelle mushrooms, which are native to the Pacific Coast, turns this classic dish into a true West Coast treat.

Smoked Salmon Pizza

When my husband and I designed and contracted our own house a few years ago, long days at the construction site destroyed, for all time, my appetite for takeout pizza. Easy homemade dough, combined with toppings like smoked salmon, curried prawns, and blue cheese (*sans* the ubiquitous tomato sauce), has since revived my interest in this classic dish.

Pizza Dough

3 cups (750 mL) all-purpose flour

2 tsp (10 mL) dry instant yeast

1 tsp (5 mL) salt

1¼ cups (310 mL) tepid water, divided

1 Tbsp (15 mL) canola oil

1 tsp (5 mL) honey

1 tsp (5 mL) canola oil, for greasing bowl

Pizza Dough

1. In a medium mixing bowl, sift the flour, and then add the yeast and salt. Whisk gently to combine.

2. Add the oil and honey to a glass measuring cup containing 1 cup (250 mL) tepid water. Stir it into the flour mixture and mix with a wooden spoon until just combined. Add the remaining ¼ cup (60 mL) water a little at a time, until the flour mixture forms a soft dough and pulls away from the sides of the bowl, adding 1 to 2 tablespoons (15 to 30 mL) more water if the dough appears dry.

3. Turn the dough out onto floured surface and knead until elastic and smooth, about 5 minutes. Place the dough in a medium greased mixing bowl, cover with a damp towel, and leave in a warm area to rise until doubled in size, about 1 hour.

4. Turn the dough back out onto the same floured surface and punch it down. Knead for 5 more minutes.

5. To make 2 thin-crust pizzas, cut the dough in half. On a large, floured cutting board, roll each half into a circle (using the board makes it easier to transfer the dough to the pizza stone). Tuck the edges underneath all the way around to form a slightly raised edge on each crust. Cover the crusts with a damp cloth and let rest until the dough starts to rise a second time, about 15 to 20 minutes.

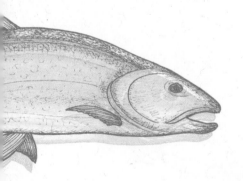

Smoked Salmon Pizza

1. Preheat the oven to 425°F (220°C). Grease 2 pizza pans lightly with cooking oil and set 1 pizza crust on each pan.
2. Spread mozzarella evenly over the crusts, and then top each pizza with half the salmon and half the onion. Sprinkle Parmesan evenly over each pizza and brush both pizzas' edges liberally with olive oil.
3. Bake until the cheese is bubbly and the edges are golden brown, about 8 to 10 minutes. Season with salt and pepper to taste and serve immediately.

Deep-dish Variation

Using the entire batch of dough for a single pizza creates a delicious "deep-dish" pizza.

On a large, floured cutting board, roll out the dough into a circle that is 2 inches (5 cm) larger than the circumference of an oven-proof cast-iron frying pan (not one with a wooden handle). Cover the dough with a damp cloth and let rise for 15 to 20 minutes.

Heat the frying pan in a preheated 425°F (220°C) oven and prepare the toppings while the pan is heating. Remove the pan from oven and brush the sides and bottom liberally with canola oil. Press the dough into the pan (the extra dough will come up the sides of the pan to create the classic deep-dish lip). Add your toppings and brush the dough edges with olive oil. Bake for 10 to 12 minutes.

Smoked Salmon Pizza

1 recipe Pizza Dough (2 crusts)
2 cups (500 mL) grated mozzarella cheese
2 cups (500 mL) flaked smoked salmon
1 medium red onion, thinly sliced
1 cup (250 mL) freshly grated Parmesan cheese
extra virgin olive oil, for brushing
salt and freshly ground pepper, to taste
Serves 4.

Wine Suggestion: Sauvignon Blanc

Dijon Salmon
with Whisky Cream Sauce

This mustard-rub/whisky-cream combo is most commonly paired with steak, but it also works well with salmon. Mustard, in fact, complements many kinds of seafood; full-flavoured fish, such as salmon, can stand up to more robust mustards like Dijon, while more delicately flavoured fish, such as halibut, is better suited to mild or grainy mustards.

1 Tbsp (15 mL) Dijon mustard
1 tsp (5 mL) coarsely ground sea salt
1 Tbsp (15 mL) crushed mixed peppercorns
4 5-oz (150 g) boneless, skinless salmon fillets
3 Tbsp (45 mL) unsalted butter, divided
1 shallot, minced
1 tsp (5 mL) flour
3 Tbsp (45 mL) whisky
1 tsp (5 mL) freshly squeezed lemon juice
½ cup (125 mL) whipping cream
1 Tbsp (15 mL) finely chopped flat-leaf parsley, for garnish

Serves 4.

Wine Suggestion: Un-oaked Chardonnay

1. Preheat the oven to 200°F (95°C). In a small bowl, whisk the Dijon mustard with the sea salt and peppercorns. Rinse the salmon fillets and dry well using paper towels. Smear the mustard rub evenly over both sides of the fish, pressing the crushed pepper very slightly into the flesh.
2. In a non-stick frying pan, melt 2 tablespoons (30 mL) butter on medium-high and sauté the fillets for 2 minutes on each side to sear the pepper-mustard rub onto the fish. Transfer the fish from the pan to a wire rack and place in the preheated oven to keep warm while you prepare the cream sauce.

3. Add 1 tablespoon (15 mL) butter and the shallot to the salmon pan and sauté on medium heat for 1 minute. Whisk in the flour, and then add the whisky and lemon juice. Continue cooking until the liquid reduces by half, and then reduce the heat to low before whisking in the whipping cream. Stirring constantly, simmer until the sauce starts to thicken, about 2 minutes.

4. Return the salmon fillets to the pan and simmer on low until the salmon is cooked through, about another minute. Arrange the salmon fillets on warmed plates, pour any remaining sauce over the fish, and garnish with parsley.

Cola-glazed Salmon

I'll admit I had my doubts about this one, but when I had half a cup of reduced Cola Glaze leftover from the previous night's ribs, I used it up on grilled salmon fillets. It was delicious: the perfect combination of sweet and hot.

Cola Glaze

1 cup (250 mL) cola

¾ cup (250 mL) dark brown sugar

¼ cup (60 mL) white wine vinegar

2 jalapeno peppers, seeded and minced

Salmon

4 7-oz (200 g) boneless salmon fillets, skin left on

2 Tbsp (30 mL) canola oil, for brushing

Serves 4.

Wine Suggestion: Pinot Noir

Cola Glaze

1. In a small saucepan, on medium-high heat, bring all the glaze ingredients to a high simmer and cook until thick and syrupy, about 30 minutes.

Salmon

1. Preheat the barbecue to medium (350°F [180°C]), clean and oil the grill, and then increase the heat to high (500°F [260°C]).
2. Rinse and dry the fish, and brush both sides of the fillets with the canola oil. Calculate the total cooking time based on 10 minutes of cooking per inch (2.5 cm) of thickness.
3. Brush the flesh side of the fillets lightly with Cola Glaze, then grill the salmon flesh side down just long enough for it to release easily from the grill, about 4 to 6 minutes, depending on the thickness of your fillets.
4. Flip the salmon and brush a generous amount of the Cola Glaze onto the flesh side of the fillets and grill until cooked through, about 4 minutes. To serve, slide a thin-lipped metal spatula between the skin and the grill, leaving the skin behind. Arrange on warm plates and serve.

Smoked Salmon Phyllo Cups

Phyllo pastry makes for a paper-thin, extra-crispy pie crust—the perfect foil for creamy oyster mushrooms and smoked salmon. Phyllo pastry dries out very rapidly, so make the filling first and keep the sheets you are not working with directly covered with a damp towel.

1. Preheat the oven to 400°F (200°C). In a medium frying pan, on medium heat, sauté the shallot in the butter until translucent. Add the mushrooms and cook until they release their liquid, about 4 minutes. Transfer the mushroom mixture to a large mixing bowl and allow it to cool to room temperature.
2. Add the crumbled salmon and the Stilton to the cooled mushrooms, and then stir to combine.
3. Brush 8 cups of a muffin tin with a little melted butter. Cut each phyllo sheet into quarters. Working on 1 cup at a time, brush 1 piece of phyllo with melted butter and mould it into the bottom of the cup. Brush a second sheet and layer it over the first sheet at a slightly different angle. Repeat with all the sheets until you have filled all the muffin cups with 4 pieces of phyllo.
4. Divide the mushroom mixture equally between the muffin cups and bake until the phyllo is golden at the edges, about 12 to 15 minutes. Serve hot.

2 Tbsp (30 mL) minced shallots

1 Tbsp (15 mL) butter, for sautéeing

3 cups (750 mL) chopped oyster mushrooms

1 cup (250 mL) crumbled smoked salmon

¾ cup (185 mL) grated Stilton cheese

8 sheets phyllo pastry

½ cup (125 mL) melted butter, for greasing and brushing

Serves 8 as a starter, or 4 for lunch.

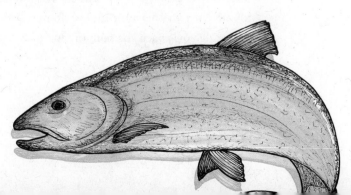

Poached Salmon with Sherry Mushroom Cream Sauce

These tasty fillets are poached in a white wine reduction, and then garnished with cream sauce. As with all poaching methods, it is important that the fish is cooked at a low simmer; cooking your fish at a rolling boil will result in overcooked, mushy, and all-around-unpleasant fish. Start this dish by preparing the sauce; it will keep quite nicely while the salmon poaches.

Sherry Mushroom Cream Sauce

1. Preheat a non-stick frying pan on medium heat and add the mushrooms. Sauté for 2 to 3 minutes, and then add the olive oil (mushrooms are very porous, and preheating both pan and mushrooms prior to adding any fat will prevent a few of the mushrooms from sucking up all of the oil). Cook the mushrooms until they release their liquid, about 5 minutes, and then transfer them to a bowl and set aside.

2. Melt the butter in the mushroom pan on medium heat. Whisk in the flour and cook until the mixture starts to brown, about 3 minutes. Add the sherry, stirring constantly; bring to a boil and reduce the amount of liquid by half. Whisk in the cream, and then stir in the mushrooms. Remove from heat and set aside while you poach the salmon.

Sherry Mushroom Cream Sauce

2 cups (500 mL) sliced fresh cremini mushrooms

1 Tbsp (15 mL) olive oil

¼ cup (60 mL) unsalted butter

2 Tbsp (30 mL) flour

½ cup (125 mL) sherry

1 cup (250 mL) whipping cream

1 tsp (5 mL) sea salt

freshly ground pepper, to taste

Poached Salmon

4 5-oz (150 g) boneless, skinless salmon fillets

2 cups (500 mL) dry white wine

1 Tbsp (15 mL) unsalted butter

Serves 4.

Wine Suggestion: Riesling

Poached Salmon

1. Rinse the salmon fillets and pat dry with paper towels. In a large frying pan, bring the white wine to a boil and reduce the liquid by half. Reduce the heat and allow the wine to cool slightly before whisking in the butter—the poaching liquid should be at a low simmer when you add the fish.

2. Add the salmon fillets, cover, and poach on medium-low heat until the flesh just starts to flake, about 10 minutes cooking time per inch (2.5 cm) of thickness (do **not** allow the liquid to boil). Drain the salmon and discard the poaching liquid.

3. Set the fillets on individual warmed plates. Briefly reheat the mushroom sauce, and then spoon it equally over the salmon.

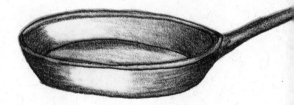

Cliffy's Notes

Mushrooms are not actually plants but the fruits of underground fungi composed of extremely thin fibres that can reach thousands of metres in length. The fungi pushes its fruits to the soil's surface by inflating them with water—which is why mushrooms sometimes appear to "spring up" overnight after a heavy rain—and the fruit reproduces by releasing spores through its gills (the corrugated lines on the bottom of the cap). Because they do not produce chlorophyll and cannot synthesize their own energy from the sun, they rely on decaying organic matter for energy.

In the kitchen, the great debate among mushroom connoisseurs is whether to wash or not to wash. On the one hand, mushrooms have a high water content and washing them can make them slimy; on the other hand, they are grown commercially in a substrate composed of wheat straw and pasteurized dry manure. I am content to brush the "dirt" off my mushrooms with a damp paper towel but my husband, who's from cow country, will not eat them unless they've been through three spin cycles in the colander. Like so many other things culinary, it's a matter of preference.

Prawns and Scallops

About Prawns

As with scallops, we eat only the large propulsion muscle of prawns (technically the abdomen, though we call it the tail), and generally discard the rest. Prawns are crustaceans and, just like their crab and lobster cousins, they are prone to spoilage from leaky digestive enzymes. However, a prawn's liver is significantly smaller than a crab's or lobster's, and it can be removed by snapping off the head (which encompasses the thorax). Keep this in mind if you are buying fresh rather than previously frozen prawns: they should either be beheaded, or **very** freshly caught.

If you are lucky enough to live on the West Coast, fresh Pacific spot prawns are the tastiest and most environmentally responsible prawns you can buy. However, most of us source our prawns frozen (raw or cooked), from our local grocery store. Frozen prawns are sold by size, and the number on the bag indicates the approximate number of prawns per pound—the smaller the number, the larger the prawn (for example, 16- to 20-count means you're getting between 16 and 20 prawns per pound).

Like all crustaceans, prawns are very susceptible to overcooking, and must be cooked at a high enough temperature to inactivate the enzymes in the muscle tissue that break down the protein and turn the meat to mush. For this reason, cook prawns for a short time at a minimum temperature of 135°F (57°C), and then serve them immediately because they do not "keep warm."

If you only have access to frozen prawns, your best choice, in terms of health and environmental impact, is to buy American-farmed white prawns; avoid farmed prawns from Asia.

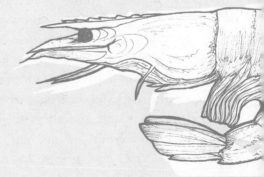

About Scallops

Scallops are actually bivalves, but in my opinion, their unique biology puts them in a culinary category that is closer to prawns than to mussels, oysters, or clams. With the exception of rock scallops, which attach themselves to rocks, scallops swim freely through the ocean, clapping their shells together as a means of propulsion. As a result, the fast-twitch part of the adductor muscle that opens and closes their shells grows large and strong, relative to other bivalves.

Unlike oysters and clams, which are generally eaten whole, only the over-sized adductor muscle is harvested from a scallop—which explains why scallops have a more consistent shape, taste, and texture than other bivalves. And, because we discard the digestive organs, scallops are one of the safest choices when it comes to eating raw shellfish.

There are more than 400 species of scallops, but they are divided by cooks into two basic categories: bay scallops and sea scallops. As their names suggest, the smaller bay scallops are gathered by divers closer to shore, while large sea scallops are dredged during off-shore commercial fishing runs that may last for weeks. The length of these runs means that the scallops are commercially processed long before they get to market—which is one reason you don't find sea scallops sold fresh in their shells. They are shucked and frozen on the boat where, because of their fragility, they are often dipped in phosphates that make them absorb water prior to freezing. This gives scallops visual appeal by making them fat and glossy, but results in an inferior product in the kitchen when all the water leaks back out into the pan. Untreated scallops are duller in appearance, but they are a superior product—and more difficult to find.

The best choices in terms of environmental impact and habitat damage are suspended aquaculture–farmed bay scallops; avoid dredged wild giant scallops.

Drunken Prawns (*en Flambé*)

This is a fun recipe that never fails to wow my kids (as in, "Wow, Mom! Your eyebrows are on fire!"). I don't have a portable gas ring, which prohibits me from performing the ultimate *en-flambé*-at-your-table trick, so I confine my pyrotechnics to the stove while the peanut gallery cheers me on from the bar stools at the kitchen island.

1. Heat a large, flame-proof frying pan on high heat. Add the butter and garlic, and sauté until fragrant, about 2 minutes (do not brown). Add the prawns and sauté until they start to turn pink, about 2 minutes (a minute longer if your prawns are large).
2. Add the brandy and light it using a long barbecue lighter. The brandy will ignite, with the flames jumping about 12 inches (30 cm). If your eyebrows are still intact, take a bow.
3. Once the flames have died down (after about 30 seconds), add the white wine and bring it to a boil, cooking until the liquid reduces by half, about 1 minute. Add the salt and pepper, reduce the heat to low, and stir in the cream. Continue stirring until the prawns are completely pink and the sauce has thickened slightly. Stir in the chives and serve immediately.

2 lb (1 kg) fresh raw prawns, shelled and de-veined
2 Tbsp (30 mL) unsalted butter
2 garlic cloves, minced
¼ cup (60 mL) brandy
2 Tbsp (30 mL) dry white wine
½ tsp (2 mL) sea salt
freshly ground pepper, to taste
3 Tbsp (45 mL) whipping cream
2 Tbsp (30 mL) minced chives
Serves 4.

Wine Suggestion: Chardonnay

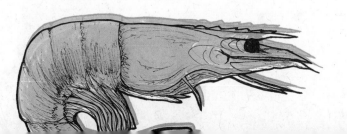

Even Drunker Scallops

Scallops in cream sauce are very often served over pasta, but I prefer to reduce the sauce to a minimum and serve this dish with a side of colourful vegetables and a loaf of fresh crusty bread.

4 Tbsp (60 mL) unsalted butter, divided
2 Tbsp (30 mL) minced white onion
1 garlic clove, minced
¾ cup (185 mL) dry white wine
⅓ cup (80 mL) cognac
½ cup (125 mL) whipping cream
2 lb (1 kg) small scallops
½ tsp (2 mL) sea salt
freshly ground pepper, to taste
Serves 4.

Wine Suggestion: Big, buttery Chardonnay

1. In a small saucepan, melt 2 tablespoons (30 mL) of the butter on medium heat. Add the onion and garlic; sauté until transparent, about 2 minutes (do not brown). Add the white wine and the cognac, bring the liquid to a boil, and reduce it by half, about 5 minutes. Whisk in the cream, and then reduce the heat to medium-low while you start the scallops.

2. Season the scallops on both sides with the salt and pepper. In a large, non-stick frying pan, melt the remaining 2 tablespoons (30 mL) butter on medium-high heat and sauté the scallops for 2 minutes.

3. Turn the scallops once, and then add the cream sauce, stirring well to deglaze the pan. Poach the scallops until just done, about 2 minutes more. Serve immediately.

Prawns Cordon Bleu

This easy, make-ahead dish works well as buffet finger food and makes a welcome alternative to shrimp cocktail.

1. In a bowl large enough to hold the prawns, whisk together the olive oil, vinegar, rosemary, and red pepper flakes. Cover the marinade and refrigerate until an hour prior to serving.
2. Rinse the prawns and pat them dry with paper towels. In a large frying pan, heat the oil on medium-high and sauté the prawns with the garlic, salt, and pepper until the prawns are pink and opaque. Drain on paper towels and refrigerate until chilled, at least 1 hour.
3. Cut the cheese into cubes small enough to fit inside the curve of each prawn. Cut the prosciutto into thin strips and wrap one strip around each cheese cube. Curl one chilled prawn around each wrapped cube and skewer it (from head to tail) with a cocktail pick or toothpick.
4. About an hour before serving, toss the prawns gently in the marinade, and then marinate them in the fridge for 30 minutes. Drain the prawns and discard the marinade. Cover and chill the prawns until serving time.

Marinade

1 cup (250 mL) olive oil

½ cup (125 mL) white wine vinegar

2 Tbsp (30 mL) minced fresh rosemary

½ tsp (2 mL) red pepper flakes

Prawns

2 lb (1 kg) large raw prawns, shelled and de-veined

3 Tbsp (45 mL) extra virgin olive oil

3 garlic cloves, minced

1 teaspoon (5 mL) sea salt

freshly ground pepper, to taste

½ lb (250 g) swiss cheese

½ lb (250 g) thinly sliced prosciutto

Serves 12 as buffet finger food, or 4 as a starter.

Prawn Marinara

If you are making marinara at the height of summer when tomatoes are at their peak, blanching, peeling, seeding, and processing fresh Romas is more than worth the effort. In the winter, when fresh tomatoes are generally awful, use good-quality, canned whole tomatoes instead.

2 lb (1 kg) peeled, seeded, and diced fresh Roma tomatoes (or substitute 1 28-oz [796 mL] can whole tomatoes, drained and chopped)

1 shallot, minced

2 garlic cloves, minced

2 Tbsp (30 mL) extra virgin olive oil

¼ tsp (1 mL) red pepper flakes

½ tsp (2 mL) coarse sea salt

freshly ground pepper, to taste

¾ lb (375 g) dried angel hair pasta

2 lb (1 kg) large raw prawns, peeled and de-veined

2 Tbsp (30 mL) chopped flat-leaf parsley, for garnishing (optional)

Serves 4.

Wine Suggestion: Chianti

1. Blanch and peel the tomatoes using the following method: with a sharp knife, cut a shallow cross into the bottom of each tomato. Using a slotted spoon, lower the tomatoes into a pan of boiling water, cook for about 10 seconds, and then transfer them to a bowl of ice water. Drain and then peel the blanched tomatoes, starting at one edge of the cross and using the edge of a paring knife to pull the skins off. Chop coarsely.

2. In a medium saucepan, on medium-low heat, sauté the shallot and garlic in the olive oil until fragrant, about 2 minutes (do not brown). Add the chopped tomatoes, salt, pepper, and red pepper flakes, and then increase the heat so the liquid from the tomatoes comes to a high simmer. Cook for 5 minutes. Remove the pan from the heat and allow the tomatoes to cool slightly, about 10 minutes.

3. Purée the cooked tomatoes using a food mill or a food processor (if you are using a food processor, strain out the seeds first, as pulverized tomato seeds are bitter and will do their best to ruin your sauce). Return the purée to the saucepan and simmer on low heat for about 15 minutes.

4. Boil a large pot of salted water and cook the pasta until it is al dente (this won't take long with angel hair pasta, so be careful not to overcook it—taste it after 3 minutes).

5. Rinse the prawns and pat them dry with paper towels. Increase the heat on the marinara sauce to medium and add the prawns to the sauce. Simmer the prawns until they turn pink and opaque, about 5 minutes, depending on their size.

6. Drain the angel hair pasta (do not rinse it), and divide it equally among four warm pasta bowls. Top the pasta with the prawn marinara, garnish with the parsley, and serve immediately.

Tips for Cooking Dried Pasta

Start by buying high-quality pasta made from durum semolina; its high protein content prevents the noodles from absorbing too much water during boiling, and keeps the cooked pasta slightly firm and chewy (otherwise known as al dente).

Use a large pot and lots of salted water—even durum semolina pasta will absorb more than one-and-a-half times its weight in water during boiling, and the water will become too starchy if you didn't have enough water initially. Salt the water using a ratio of 1 teaspoon (5 mL) of salt per quart (litre) of water, and bring it to a rolling boil before adding the noodles. The salt will limit the starch's ability to gel, and the agitation of the rolling boil will help to keep the strands physically apart.

Taste a strand after 4 minutes of cooking (3 minutes for angel hair), and every minute after that, until the noodles are cooked to your taste. Drain them in a colander, but do not rinse them: rinsing off the residual starch will prevent your sauce from sticking to your noodles.

Scallops Poached in Orange Butter

Scallops are naturally high in glucose and their sweetness makes a natural match for sweet aromatics, including oranges.

½ tsp (2 mL) coriander seeds
¼ cup (60 mL) unsalted butter
1 tsp (5 mL) orange zest
½ cup (125 mL) freshly squeezed orange juice
3 Tbsp (45 mL) Curaçao liqueur
· 2 lb (1 kg) small scallops

Serves 4.

Wine Suggestion: Riesling

1. Coarsely crush the coriander seeds using a mortar and pestle, or the side of a large chef's knife. In a small saucepan, melt the butter on low heat, add the coriander and orange zest and cook for 5 minutes.
2. Whisk the orange juice into the melted butter, and then remove the pan from the heat and whisk in the Curaçao.
3. Rinse the scallops and pat them dry with paper towels. Transfer the Orange Butter to a large skillet and bring the mixture to a bare simmer on medium-low heat.
4. Add the scallops, cover, and poach them until just opaque in the centre, turning once (about 5 minutes total, depending on thickness). Divide the scallops between 4 pre-warmed plates, drizzle with the remaining Orange Butter and serve immediately.

Lemon Prawn Kebabs

When skewering prawns for grilling, use half moon–shaped metal skewers and pierce the prawns lengthwise, from head to tail.

1. In a medium mixing bowl, whisk together all the marinade ingredients and set aside.
2. Rinse the prawns and pat dry with paper towels. Add them to the marinade, and gently toss to coat on all sides. Cover and refrigerate for a maximum of 30 minutes.
3. Preheat the barbecue to medium (350°F [180°C]), clean and oil the grill, and then increase the heat to high (500°F [260°C]).
4. Cut 1 lemon into thick slices, and then cut each slice into quarters.
5. Drain the prawns on paper towels and discard the marinade. Thread the prawns onto 8 medium metal skewers, alternating each prawn with a piece of lemon. Grill on high heat, turning once, until the prawns are pink and opaque, about 4 minutes total. Cut the other lemon into fresh wedges and serve alongside the prawns.

Marinade

2 Tbsp (30 mL) dry white wine

1 Tbsp (15 mL) extra virgin olive oil

2 garlic cloves, minced

zest of 1 lemon

2 Tbsp (30 mL) freshly squeezed lemon juice

1 bay leaf

1 tsp (5 mL) sea salt

Prawns

2 lb (1 kg) large raw prawns, shelled and de-veined

2 lemons

Serves 4.

Wine Suggestion: White Burgundy

Prawns Vindaloo
with Cucumber Raita

Although vindaloo is now considered to be an Indian dish, it was originally brought by the Portuguese to the Goan region of India, where it evolved from a wine and garlic pork dish into a spicy chicken or lamb dish served for special occasions. Traditional vindaloo dishes are extremely hot, but serving the dish with a cooling cucumber raita (yogurt-based dip) will help to cool your palate.

Garam Masala

2 tsp (10 mL) cardamon seeds

2 tsp (10 mL) black peppercorns

2 tsp (10mL) cumin seeds

2 tsp (10 mL) coriander seeds

6 whole cloves

2 tsp (10 mL) mustard seeds

2-inch (5 cm) piece of cinnamon stick

Cucumber Raita

1 cup (250 mL) plain yogurt (you will get a creamier product if you use full-fat yogurt)

1 medium field cucumber, peeled, seeded, and chopped

¼ cup (60 mL) chopped white onion

1 garlic clove, chopped

2 Tbsp (30 mL) chopped fresh mint leaves

½ tsp (2.5 mL) salt

fresh mint leaves, for garnishing

Garam Masala

1. Heat a cast-iron frying pan on medium-low heat. Add all the spices and dry-roast for 15 minutes, stirring frequently. Remove from pan and cool completely, about 15 minutes.

2. On a shatterproof surface (not, for example, your granite countertop), wrap the cinnamon stick in a clean dishcloth and break it into small pieces with a hammer. Place the broken cinnamon and the rest of the spices in a spare coffee grinder (do not use your regular coffee grinder or your coffee will taste like curry), and grind into a consistent powder. Stored in a cool, dark place, in an airtight container, it will keep for a couple of months.

Cucumber Raita

1. In a blender or food processor, combine the yogurt, ¼ cup (60 mL) cold water, cucumber, onion, garlic, and chopped mint leaves and process until smooth.

2. Transfer the mixture to a large serving bowl, garnish with fresh mint leaves, cover with plastic wrap, and refrigerate until needed.

Prawns Vindaloo

1. Cook the rice according to the package directions (which should be equal to the time it takes you to prepare the vindaloo).
2. Rinse the prawns and pat dry on paper towels, and then set aside.
3. In a large cast-iron frying pan, heat the canola oil on medium heat. Add the onion, garlic, ginger, and chili pepper, and sauté until the mixture starts to brown, about 5 minutes. Add the Garam Masala, fenugreek seeds, chili powder, mustard seeds, and salt, and sauté for another 2 to 3 minutes.
4. Add the wine vinegar and ¼ cup (60 mL) water, reduce the heat to low, and simmer for about 15 minutes to blend the flavours.
5. Increase the heat to medium-high, add the prawns, and sauté until they turn completely pink, about 4 minutes (a minute longer if you have larger prawns). Serve immediately over the rice, with Cucumber Raita on the side.

Prawns Vindaloo

2 cups (500 mL) basmati rice

3 lb (1.5 kg) large raw prawns, shelled and de-veined

2 Tbsp (30 mL) canola oil

1 medium onion, diced

2 garlic cloves, minced

1 Tbsp (15 mL) grated fresh ginger

1 hot chili pepper of your choice, seeded and chopped

2 Tbsp (30 mL) Garam Masala (p. 104)

1 tsp (5 mL) fenugreek seeds

1 Tbsp (15 mL) chili powder

2 tsp (10 mL) whole mustard seeds

½ tsp (2.5 mL) salt

2 Tbsp (30 mL) red wine vinegar

Serves 4.

Wine Suggestion: Riesling

Ted's Firecracker Prawns

My husband, Ted, invented this dish to use up the odd assortment of mismatched prawns we had in the freezer when we didn't have enough of any one kind for a "regular" recipe. It was so good that I now mix and match prawns and marinades on purpose.

Prawns

½ lb (250 g) large raw prawns, shelled and de-veined

½ lb (250 g) pre-cooked frozen prawns

Spicy Marinade

2 Tbsp (30 mL) Chinese hoisin sauce

1 Tbsp (15 mL) soy sauce

1 tsp (5 mL) Hunan red chili paste (or substitute sambal oelek)

Fish Marinade

1 Tbsp (15 mL) bottled fish sauce

1 Tbsp (15 mL) pale dry sherry

freshly ground pepper

Stir-fry

¼ cup (60 mL) cornstarch

2 Tbsp (30 mL) peanut oil

2 garlic cloves, chopped

1 Tbsp (15 mL) chopped green onion

2 hot chili peppers of your choice, seeded and sliced

1 tsp (5 mL) soy sauce

2 Tbsp (30 mL) chopped cilantro, for garnishing

Serves 4 as an appetizer, or 2 as a main course.

Beer Suggestion: Cold lager

1. Thaw and rinse all the prawns and pat dry using paper towels.
2. In medium bowl, whisk together the ingredients for the Spicy Marinade. Add the raw prawns, cover, and marinate for 20 minutes in the fridge.
3. In a second medium bowl, whisk together the ingredients for the Fish Marinade. Add the pre-cooked prawns, cover, and marinate for 20 minutes in the fridge.
4. Remove the prawns from their respective marinades and drain on paper towels, discarding the marinades.
5. Place the cornstarch in a plastic bag and add the raw prawns; shake gently until the prawns are coated on all sides.
6. In a well-seasoned cast-iron frying pan, heat the oil until it is very hot (but not smoking), and add the cornstarch-coated prawns. Sauté until the prawns have mostly turned pink, about 3 minutes.
7. Add the cooked prawns, garlic, green onion, and chili peppers. Sauté until the raw prawns have turned completely pink and opaque, and the cooked prawns are heated through, about 2 minutes. Stir in the remaining soy sauce, garnish with the cilantro and serve.

Cliffy's Notes

One way to control the heat in a spicy dish is through your choice of chili pepper. The heat in peppers is measured in Scoville heat units (SHU), and is dependent on the amount of capsaicin produced by the variety in question: the more capsaicin, the hotter the pepper. Bell peppers, for instance, have a recessive gene that prevents them from producing any capsaicin at all so they measure 0 SHU. At the other end of the scale are habaneros, with an average score of about 350,000 SHU. The common jalapeno is mild by comparison, registering a mere 10,000 SHU (and, in case you ever get arrested, it might interest you to know that police-grade pepper spray tops the scale at over 5,000,000 SHU).

Blue Cheese Linguine
with Prawns

This very basic dish is rich enough to feel like a treat, but without the effort and prep time. It's the perfect comfort food in the middle of an Alberta blizzard when I've shovelled my driveway 15 times in 3 days and can afford the extra calories.

¾ lb (375 g) dried linguine pasta

¼ cup (60 mL) unsalted butter

2 lb (1 kg) large raw prawns, shelled and de-veined

1 cup (250 mL) whipping cream

½ cup (125 mL) freshly grated Parmesan cheese

¼ cup (60 mL) crumbled blue cheese

1 tsp (5 mL) salt

freshly ground pepper, to taste

2 Tbsp (30 mL) minced flat-leaf parsley, for garnishing

Serves 4.

Wine Suggestion: Pinot Gris

1. Bring a large pot of salted water to a furious boil and cook the linguine. Taste it after 4 minutes, and then again every minute until it's cooked to your taste. Drain and set aside.
2. In a large saucepan, melt the butter on medium-high heat and sauté the prawns for 2 minutes. Gradually stir in the whipping cream and cook until the prawns are pink and opaque, about 3 more minutes.
3. Reduce the heat to low and add the cooked linguine to the prawns and sauce. Toss to coat, and then stir in the Parmesan, blue cheese, salt, and pepper. Divide between 4 warmed pasta bowls, sprinkle with the parsley, and serve immediately.

Pan-seared Scallops with Cognac Butter

The trick to properly seared scallops is heat. If your pan isn't hot enough, the scallops end up being poached instead of seared—still good, but without the delicious buttery crust on the outside.

1. Rinse the scallops and dry them very well with paper towels. In a well-seasoned cast-iron frying pan, heat the canola oil on high until it is very hot (but not smoking—the smoke from burning cooking oil is toxic).

2. Add the scallops to the pan 2 at a time, waiting about 30 seconds between batches (overloading the pan with cold seafood will drastically reduce the temperature in the pan). Once they start to sizzle, resist the urge to move the scallops around in the pan. Let them sit in the same spot for 2 to 3 minutes, depending on their thickness, before flipping them *once* (again, do the pairs 30 seconds apart). Sear the second side for 1 more minute. The scallops should still be springy in the middle—stiff scallops are overcooked.

3. Remove the scallops from the pan and drain on paper towels. Add the butter and the cognac to the pan, stirring well to get the brown bits off the bottom.

4. Place the scallops on 4 small pre-warmed plates, drizzle them with the Cognac Butter, and serve immediately.

3 Tbsp (45 mL) canola oil
8 large sea scallops
1 Tbsp (15 mL) unsalted butter
2 Tbsp (30 mL) cognac
Serves 4 as a starter.

Wine Suggestion: Chardonnay

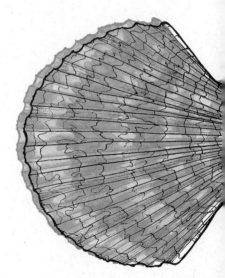

Garlic Prawns

Years ago, I tried the late James Barber's suggestion of washing my hands in cold water after handling garlic in order to keep its pungent odour out of my skin. It worked—unlike his recipe for roasting a chicken with 40 cloves of garlic, which nearly got me evicted from my apartment. Even now, any recipe involving more than half-a-dozen cloves of garlic reminds me of his *Urban Peasant* approach to cooking.

2 Tbsp (30 mL) butter
2 Tbsp (30 mL) extra virgin olive oil
1 shallot, diced
6 large garlic cloves, minced
½ tsp (2 mL) salt
freshly ground pepper, to taste
zest from 1 medium lemon
2 lb (1 kg) large prawns, shelled and de-veined
freshly squeezed juice from 1 medium lemon
2 Tbsp (30 mL) minced green onion
Serves 4.

Wine Suggestion: Sauvignon Blanc

1. In a large frying pan, melt the butter and the olive oil on medium heat. Add the shallot and sauté until translucent, about 2 minutes. Add the garlic, salt, pepper, and lemon zest and sauté until fragrant, about 2 minutes (do not brown).
2. Add the prawns and sauté for 3 minutes. Stir in the lemon juice and cook until the prawns turn pink and opaque, about 2 minutes more, depending on their size. Stir in the green onion and serve immediately.

Prawn-stuffed Tomatoes

The tang of lime contrasts with the unctuous mouth-feel of avocado, creating the perfect complement to these easy, make-ahead prawn-stuffed tomatoes. As with guacamole, you'll get a nicer texture if you dice, rather than mash, the avocados.

1. Slice the tomatoes lengthwise into halves; scoop out and discard the pulp.
2. In a medium mixing bowl, combine the diced prawns, cilantro, green onion, and lime juice.
3. Peel and dice the avocados and gently stir them into the diced prawns. Spoon the mixture into the tomato halves and top each one with a whole, chilled prawn. Cover and refrigerate until ready to serve.

12 small, perfectly ripe plum tomatoes

½ lb (250 g) cooked prawns, peeled and diced

¼ cup (60 mL) minced cilantro

¼ cup (60 mL) minced green onion

freshly squeezed juice from 1 lime

2 medium avocados

24 small whole cooked prawns, peeled, de-veined, and chilled

Serves 12 as buffet finger food.

Peel-and-eat Pan-fried Prawns

If you are lucky enough to have access to freshly caught Pacific spot prawns with the heads and legs still on, keep your recipe simple and your seasonings to a minimum so you can savour the taste and texture of the prawns themselves.

Peel-and-eat Prawns with Hot Sauce

5 lb (2.2 kg) freshly caught spot prawns, heads and tails still on

¼ cup (60 mL) unsalted butter

3 Tbsp (45 mL) Frank's Red Hot Sauce (or substitute your favourite hot sauce)

2 limes, cut into wedges

Serves 4.

Wine Suggestion: Gewürztraminer

Peel-and-eat Prawns with Hot Sauce

1. Snap the heads off the prawns and pull off the legs with your fingers. To "butterfly" each prawn, run a sharp knife down the length of the back, cutting through the shell and about halfway into the flesh. Flatten the prawn gently with the palm of your hand. Use the tip of the knife to hook and pull out the black "vein" found at the head end of the prawn (which is the end of the prawn's intestine).

2. In a large frying pan, melt the butter on medium-high heat and sauté the prawns for 3 minutes. Stir in the hot sauce and sauté until the prawns are pink and opaque, about 2 minutes, depending on their size. Serve immediately with lime wedges on the side.

Peel-and-eat Salt and Pepper Prawns

1. Prepare the prawns as described on the previous page. Crack the peppercorns using a mortar and pestle, or use the side of a large chef's knife.

2. In a large cast-iron frying pan, heat the oil on high until it shimmers (but doesn't smoke) and sauté the prawns until they are pink and opaque, about 4 minutes, depending on their size. Add the salt and pepper and toss to coat. Serve immediately with lemon wedges.

Peel-and-eat Salt and Pepper Prawns

5 lb (2.2 kg) freshly caught spot prawns, heads and tails still on

2 Tbsp (30 mL) peppercorns

¼ cup (60 mL) canola oil

2 Tbsp (30 mL) coarse sea salt

2 lemons, cut into wedges

Serves 4.

Beer Suggestion: Cold lager

West Coast Paella

While it seems that no two cooks agree on the exact ingredients that constitute "authentic" paella, there is a general consensus that the addition of saffron, the world's most expensive spice, is crucial to both the colour and flavour of this dish.

3 Tbsp (45 mL) olive oil

1 medium onion, chopped

3 garlic cloves, minced

½ lb (250 g) hot Italian sausage, cut into 1-inch (2.5 cm) chunks

1 lb (500 g) chicken breast, cut into bite-size pieces

1 cup (250 mL) uncooked short-grain rice (Arborio works well)

½ lb (250 g) squid, cut into pieces (optional)

1 pinch saffron strands

3 cups (750 mL) chicken stock

½ lb (250 g) raw prawns, peeled and de-veined

1 red bell pepper, sliced into thin strips

1 large ripe tomato, chopped

½ cup (125 mL) green peas, fresh or frozen

½ lb (250 g) live mussels, in the shell

½ lb (250 g) live clams, in the shell

Serves 4.

Wine Suggestion: Rosé

1. In a large cast-iron frying pan, heat the oil on medium heat. Add the onion and sauté until transparent, about 2 minutes. Add the garlic and the sausage chunks. Sauté for 2 minutes, and then add the chicken pieces. Stirring frequently, cook until the chicken and sausage are browned. Add the rice to the pan and stir vigorously until the rice turns translucent, about 5 minutes.
2. Stir in the squid (if using), saffron, and stock; cover and simmer until the meat and rice are cooked, about 20 minutes.
3. Stir the prawns, red pepper, tomato, and peas into the rice mixture. Cover and cook until the prawns are completely pink.
4. In a separate pan, steam the mussels and clams in ½ cup (125 mL) water for 5 minutes until they are all open, **discarding any that remain closed.** Drain the shellfish, add them to the paella, and serve immediately.

Cliffy's Notes

Paella—named for the pan in which this dish is traditionally cooked—is probably Spain's most famous dish, but contrary to popular belief, this peasant dish was not originally a seafood dish because the labourers who invented it did not have access to much seafood. Instead, they used whatever they could grow, raise, or hunt, and the oldest versions of this dish used everything from snails to rabbits to wild fowl.

Scallop and Asparagus Salad

Whether served hot or cold, scallops pair remarkably well with asparagus. Served alfresco with a chilled bottle of Chablis on a hot August day, these chilled poached scallops make a great Sunday lunch.

2 Tbsp (30 mL) unsalted butter
2 Tbsp (30 mL) minced shallot
2 garlic cloves, minced
¼ cup (125 mL) dry white wine
1 lb (500 g) small (bay) scallops
ice cold water, in a large bowl
1 lb (500 g) fresh asparagus spears
freshly squeezed juice from 1 medium orange
1 Tbsp plus 1 tsp (20 mL) sesame oil
1 Tbsp (15 mL) rice vinegar
1 Tbsp (15 mL) toasted sesame seeds

Serves 4.

Wine Suggestion: Chablis

1. Heat a large, non-stick frying pan on medium heat. Add the butter, shallot, and garlic, and sauté until fragrant, about 2 minutes (do not brown). Add the white wine and bring the liquid to a simmer (do not boil). Add the scallops, cover, and poach until just cooked, about 3 minutes (if your scallops are large, they may take a minute more).

2. Remove the scallops from the poaching liquid and plunge them immediately into ice cold water to stop them from cooking. Drain on paper towels and set aside while you make the salad.

3. Wash the asparagus and snap off any woody ends (peeling the bottom of the stalks is optional). Steam the asparagus in an upright vegetable steamer, or boil it, uncovered, in a wide, shallow pan until it is tender-crisp, about 5 minutes. Plunge the asparagus into ice cold water to stop it from cooking. Drain and set aside.

4. In a small bowl, whisk together the orange juice, sesame oil, and rice vinegar.

5. Divide the asparagus evenly between 4 plates and top with the scallops. Drizzle the dressing over each salad and sprinkle with the toasted sesame seeds. Serve immediately.

Tips for Buying Asparagus

More so than any other vegetable, asparagus tastes far superior when you buy it locally and in season. Asparagus is the new spring growth of a type of lily plant and the immature shoots continue to grow even after harvest, consuming most of their own sugar within 24 hours of being picked. As the sugar is depleted, the shoots become fibrous and lose their sweetness. Early spring asparagus is high in sugar (about 4%), but as the season progresses, the plant's stored energy becomes gradually exhausted and the asparagus stalks have less sugar as a result.

When buying asparagus, choose bright green stalks with tightly closed tips. The bunch should feel heavy in your hand when you pick it up. Do not buy asparagus if the tips have started to open or the stems are flat and/or wrinkled. As long as the asparagus has been freshly harvested, the thickness of the stalks is a matter of personal preference, although peeling the bottom half of very thick stalks will allow them to cook more evenly.

To store asparagus, place it upright in a glass with an inch or two of diluted sugar water (1 teaspoon [5 mL] sugar per ½ cup [125 mL] water).

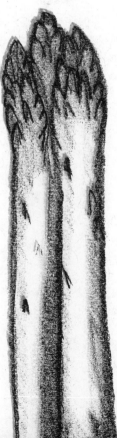

Coconut Prawns

"Butterflying" these prawns prior to coating them maximizes the surface area for the shredded coconut and creates an extra crispy coating.

Batter
¾ cup (185 mL) cornstarch
¼ cup (60 mL) flour
1 tsp (5 mL) baking powder
1 tsp (5 mL) salt
1 egg
Prawns
2 lb (1 kg) raw prawns, peeled and de-veined
1 cup (250 mL) flour, spread on a plate
2 cups (500 mL) shredded sweet coconut, spread on a plate
½ cup (125 mL) canola oil, for frying
Serves 4.

Wine Suggestion: Sauvignon Blanc

Batter

1. In a medium mixing bowl, whisk together the cornstarch, flour, baking powder, and salt. In a smaller bowl, lightly beat the egg with ¼ cup (60 mL) water, and then add it to the cornstarch mixture. Cover and chill for about half an hour.

Prawns

1. Rinse the prawns and pat dry with paper towels. Butterfly each prawn by running a sharp knife the length of its back, cutting about halfway through the flesh (be careful not to cut too deep—you want the prawn to stay in one piece). Lay the prawn on a cutting board and press gently with your palm to flatten it slightly.
2. Coat each prawn in the flour, shaking off the excess (this will help the batter to stick). Dip each prawn in the batter, and then roll it in the coconut until completely coated. Set the prawns on a wire rack (placed over a baking sheet to catch any drips).
3. In a large, well-seasoned cast-iron frying pan, heat the oil on high until very hot (but not smoking). Pan-fry the prawns in a single layer but do not crowd the pan. Turn the prawns once, and cook until the coating is crisp and the prawns are fully cooked, about 3 minutes total. Drain very briefly on paper towels and serve piping hot with Cocktail Sauce on the side.

Cocktail Sauce

1. In a small saucepan on medium heat, whisk together the tomato paste, lemon juice, brown sugar, Worcestershire sauce, Tabasco, and salt. Reduce the heat to low, cover, and simmer for 10 minutes. Remove from heat and allow the sauce to cool completely.

2. Whisk in the horseradish, cover, and refrigerate until needed. Stored in an airtight container, it will keep for about a week. **Note:** if you use a mild creamy horseradish, you will need to use more of it to get the same "bite," which will make the sauce pink and anemic-looking (though it will still taste good). To keep the sauce looking vibrant, either use Homemade Horseradish (p. 140), or use a hot, non-creamy bottled variety.

Cocktail Sauce

1 cup (250 mL) tomato paste

2 Tbsp (30 mL) freshly squeezed lemon juice

2 Tbsp (30 mL) brown sugar

2 tsp (10 mL) Worcestershire sauce

1 tsp (5 mL) Tabasco sauce (or to taste)

½ tsp (2 mL) salt

2 Tbsp (45 mL) prepared hot horseradish (not creamed)

Makes 1 cup (250 mL).

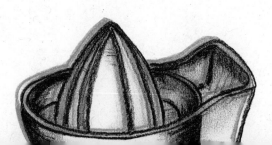

Halibut

About Halibut

The largest of all the flatfish, Pacific halibut can reach weights of over 700 pounds (315 kilograms), and its Latin name, *Hippoglossus stenolepis*, translates as "hippo of the sea." Interestingly, juvenile halibuts start life torpedo-shaped, like salmon, with one eye on either side of their heads but, after a few months, the left eye migrates over to the right side, the pigmentation on the left side fades to white, and the fish subsequently changes its orientation in the water. They become voracious carnivores and use camouflage to avoid detection from their prey: viewed from above, their dark, mottled tops allow them to blend seamlessly into the ocean floor, and their white bellies obscure their outlines against the bright surface of the water when seen from below.

Halibut has mild-tasting, firm white flesh that is low in fat, and has the culinary advantage of having very few bones. It is available fresh from March through November, and, properly wrapped, it will freeze well for several months.

Because of their large size, halibut steaks are cut close to the tail and the main part of the body is cut into fillets. The cheeks, considered a delicacy, are removed and sold separately. As with all seafood, source this fish from a reputable fishmonger or a grocery store with a high turnover and clean, glass-covered display cases. Whole halibut is rarely available commercially, but if you are interested in cooking a whole fish, you may be able to special order a "chicken" (less than 20 pounds [9 kilograms]), from a cannery or specialty fishmonger.

In terms of sustainability, longline-harvested Pacific halibut are the best choice; avoid trawl-harvested Atlantic halibut and flounder.

Halibut Ceviche

Although the texture of the halibut in this recipe is transformed by the acid, the fish is technically classified by Health Canada as "raw," which means that any seafood you use in a ceviche must be of the highest quality. While pathogens, such as salmonella, listeria, and E. coli, to name but a few, are destroyed by heat, they are not destroyed by an acidic marinade; safe storage and food-handling practices are absolutely imperative for this recipe.

1½ lb (750 g) boneless, skinless halibut fillets, cut into bite-size chunks

1 large white onion, peeled and chopped

2 cups (500 mL) lime juice

1 jalapeno pepper, seeded and minced

1 red bell pepper, chopped

1 large tomato, chopped

3 green onions, chopped

3 Tbsp (45 mL) minced cilantro

½ tsp (2 mL) sea salt

freshly squeezed juice from 1 large orange

2 avocados, peeled and sliced

Serves 8 as a starter, or 4 for lunch.

Wine Suggestion: Sauvignon Blanc

1. In a non-reactive (glass) bowl, combine the halibut chunks with the white onion and the lime juice, cover and refrigerate for 4 to 5 hours. Drain the fish and discard the marinade.
2. In a non-reactive (glass) serving bowl, combine the jalapeno, red pepper, tomato, green onion, cilantro, orange juice, and salt. Stir in the halibut, being careful not to break up the fish chunks. Garnish with the avocado and serve chilled.

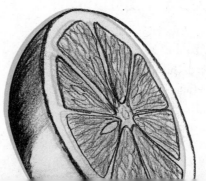

Cliffy's Notes

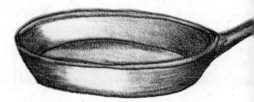

Heat is not the only way to "cook" seafood. Raw fish flesh is made of basic proteins that are wound up like the curly ribbon on a Christmas present. These proteins are spaced far enough apart that light can squeeze between them, which is why fish has a shiny, translucent appearance. Heat changes the physical structure of these proteins so that they unwind (denature) and stick together (coagulate). This causes the translucent fish muscle to become solid and firm, what we commonly call "cooked."

Acid, however, will also cause fish protein to denature and coagulate, and in many coastal areas (where inhabitants had limited access to cooking fuel but unlimited access to fruit), a traditional way to "cook" seafood is to marinate it in citric acid, along with onions and chili peppers. "Cooking" halibut in this way results in a firm and opaque fish—only without the roasting and browning flavours we associate with heat.

Blackened Halibut

To "blacken" the halibut, the hot spice mix chars with the milk solids in the butter to create a dark crust on the outside, and a parcel of tender fish on the inside.

Spice Paste

3 garlic cloves, minced

1 tsp (5 mL) paprika

½ tsp (2 mL) crushed red pepper flakes

½ tsp (2 mL) cayenne pepper

½ tsp (2 mL) dried thyme

½ tsp (2 mL) dried oregano

1 tsp (5 mL) salt

freshly ground pepper, to taste

2 Tbsp (30 mL) melted butter

2 Tbsp (30 mL) freshly squeezed lime juice

Halibut

4 halibut fillets, 1 inch (2.5 cm) thick

2 limes, cut into wedges

Serves 4.

Beer Suggestion: Cold lager

1. In a small mixing bowl, blend together all the ingredients for the spice paste.
2. Rinse the halibut fillets and pat them dry with paper towels. Spread a thin layer of the paste over both sides of the fish, cover with plastic wrap, and refrigerate for 30 minutes.
3. Preheat the barbecue to medium (350°F [180°C]), clean and oil the grill, and then increase the heat to high (500°F [260°C]). Grill the fillets for a total cooking time of 10 minutes, flipping once, a little more than halfway through the cooking. Serve immediately with lime wedges

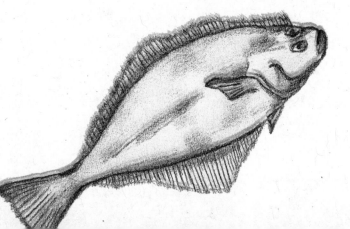

Grilled Halibut
with Anchovy Butter

Anchovies are small herring-like fish that are harvested from the Mediterranean and cured in salt for up to 10 months. After curing, they are often filleted, repacked in olive oil, and sold in small cans (typically 2 ounces [60 grams]). Whole anchovies packed in their original salt can also be found at specialty markets. Anchovies are usually mashed to a paste and added to sauces and dressings to augment their flavour.

1. Drain the anchovy fillets on paper towels. In a small bowl, mash them into a smooth paste using the back of a fork.
2. In a medium mixing bowl, cream the butter, and then add the anchovy paste, lemon juice, and cayenne pepper. Cream until fully combined, cover and refrigerate in an airtight container until needed. (If you used freshly opened anchovies, this butter will keep for about a week.)
3. Preheat the barbecue to medium (350°F [180°C]), clean and oil the grill, and then increase the heat to high (500°F [260°C]). Rinse the steaks, pat them dry with paper towels, and then brush both sides with the melted butter.
4. Grill the fish, turning once, based on 10 minutes total cooking time per inch (2.5 cm) of thickness. Grill the first side a little longer (about 6 minutes for 1-inch [2.5 cm] steaks), and then 3 to 4 minutes on the second side, until the fish is completely opaque.
5. Set the steaks on 4 pre-warmed plates, spoon 1 tablespoon (15 mL) of the anchovy butter onto each steak, and serve.

½ cup (125 mL) unsalted butter, at room temperature

4 canned anchovy fillets

1 tsp (5 mL) freshly squeezed lemon juice

¼ tsp (1 mL) cayenne pepper

4 6-oz (175 g) halibut steaks, at least 1 inch (2.5 cm) thick

2 Tbsp (30 mL) melted butter, for brushing

Serves 4.

Wine Suggestion: Pinot Grigio

Halibut Cheeks with Basil-Tomato Salad

With the texture of crabmeat and the sweet taste of scallops, halibut cheeks are, arguably, the most succulent part of halibut. They can occasionally be found fresh at upscale seafood markets, but are more commonly available (flash frozen and vacuum packed) at canneries and online. If you see them for sale, they are well worth the price.

2 lb (1 kg) halibut cheeks
½ tsp (2 mL) sea salt
freshly ground pepper, to taste
3 Tbsp (45 mL) canola oil
1 medium red onion
1 Tbsp (15 mL) olive oil, for brushing
2 lb (1 kg) vine-ripened tomatoes
½ cup (125 mL) torn fresh basil (not chopped)
¼ cup (60 mL) extra virgin olive oil
2 Tbsp (30 mL) freshly squeezed lemon juice
1 tsp (5 mL) coarse sea salt
freshly cracked black pepper, to taste
Serves 4.

Wine Suggestion: Pinot Grigio

1. If starting with frozen cheeks, thaw completely before cooking. Season the cheeks on both sides with salt and pepper, and let them rest for 15 or 20 minutes.
2. Pat the halibut cheeks with paper towels to remove any moisture brought to the surface by the salt, and then place in a bowl with the canola oil. Stir gently to coat the cheeks with the oil.
3. Preheat the barbecue to medium (350°F [180°C]), clean and oil the grill, and then increase the heat to high (500°F [260°C]). Peel and cut the onion into thick slices, and then brush both sides of each slice with the olive oil. Cook directly on the grill until they just start to char, about 3 minutes. Remove from the heat and set aside to cool.

4. Rinse the tomatoes, cut them into wedges and place them in a large serving bowl. Separate the cooled onion into individual rings and add it to the tomatoes, along with the basil, extra virgin olive oil, lemon juice, salt, and pepper. Toss gently.
5. Cook the halibut cheeks directly on the grill, cooking the first side for about three-quarters of the total cooking time, about 5 minutes. When the cheeks are almost opaque, turn them once and grill until just cooked, about 1 more minute. Arrange the halibut on top of the salad and serve immediately.

Jerked Halibut
with Pineapple Salsa

Traditional Jamaican jerk seasoning calls for scotch bonnet peppers, which are extremely hot. You can reduce the heat in this dish by substituting jalapeno peppers. Prepare the salsa a few hours in advance so that the grilled pineapple has enough time to chill and the flavours have a chance to blend.

Pineapple Salsa

1 medium fresh pineapple, peeled and cored
1 Tbsp (15 mL) canola oil
1 tsp (5 mL) honey
1 medium red onion, diced
1 small jalapeno pepper, seeded and diced
1 small red bell pepper, seeded and diced
freshly squeezed juice from 1 lime
1 tsp (5 mL) coarse sea salt
freshly ground pepper, to taste
3 Tbsp (45 mL) coarsely chopped cilantro

Jerk Seasoning

1 scotch bonnet (or jalapeno) pepper
1 small white onion, chopped
4 green onions, sliced
2 garlic cloves, chopped
2 Tbsp (30 mL) brown sugar
1 tbsp (15 mL) minced fresh thyme
(or 1 tsp [5mL] dried thyme)
1 tsp (5 mL) ground allspice
½ tsp (2 mL) ground cinnamon
½ tsp (2 mL) ground nutmeg
¼ tsp (1 mL) ground cloves
3 Tbsp (45 mL) canola oil
3 Tbsp (45 mL) soy sauce

Pineapple Salsa

1. Preheat the barbecue to medium (350°F [180°C]), and clean and oil the grill. Peel and core the pineapple, and slice it into thick rings. In a small bowl, whisk the canola oil into the honey and brush this mixture on both sides of the pineapple rings. Grill the pineapple on medium heat, turning once, until the fruit begins to blacken, about 5 minutes total.

2. Remove the rings from the heat and allow them to cool completely, about 20 minutes.

3. In a medium bowl, combine the remaining salsa ingredients. Dice the cooled pineapple and add it to the bowl. Stir to combine, cover, and refrigerate until serving.

Jerk Seasoning

1. For a milder seasoning, remove the seeds and membranes from the hot pepper prior to processing. (If you go with the scotch bonnet pepper, it's a good idea to wear gloves while handling it; be vigilant about not touching your eyes or face while preparing this recipe.) Place all the jerk seasoning ingredients in a food processor and blend to combine.

Halibut

1. Rinse the fish and pat dry with paper towels. Arrange the fillets in a shallow glass baking dish and coat both sides with Jerk Seasoning. Cover with plastic wrap and refrigerate for 1 hour.

2. Preheat the barbecue to medium (350°F [180°C]), clean and oil the grill, and then increase the heat to high (500°F [260°C]). In a smoking box (or aluminum loaf pan with holes punched in the bottom), dampen the wood chips, and then set directly on the grill.

3. Add the halibut to the grill and cook on high heat, allowing 10 minutes cooking time per inch (2.5 cm) of thickness. Turn once, about three-quarters of the way through the total cooking time. Slide the fish off the grill onto warmed plates using a thin-lipped metal spatula. Serve immediately with Pineapple Salsa.

Jerked Halibut

4 8-oz (250 g) halibut fillets
1 recipe Jerk Seasoning (p. 128)
food-grade wood chips, for smoking
(or your own made from untreated lumber)
Serves 4.

Beer Suggestion: Cold lager

Halibut Provençal

The cuisine of Provence, in the south of France, use commonly available Mediterranean basin ingredients, including olive oil, garlic, tomatoes, and herbs—all of which pair very nicely with halibut.

4 5-oz (150 g) boneless, skinless halibut fillets

3 garlic cloves

¼ cup plus 2 Tbsp (90 mL) extra virgin olive oil, divided

2 Tbsp (30 mL) lemon juice

½ tsp (2 mL) coarse salt

freshly ground pepper, to taste

1 lb (500 g) fresh Roma tomatoes

1 small onion, diced

1 garlic clove, minced

½ tsp (2 mL) dried oregano

¼ tsp (1 mL) dried thyme

½ cup (125 mL) dry white wine

Serves 4.

Wine Suggestion: Sauvignon Blanc

1. Rinse the halibut fillets and pat dry with paper towels.
2. Squash the garlic cloves with the side of a large chef's knife to pop them out of their skins, then squash them a few more times to release the oil. In a heavy-duty resealable freezer bag, combine the garlic with ¼ cup (60 mL) of the olive oil, and lemon juice, salt, and pepper. Seal the bag and swish to combine the marinade ingredients. Add the halibut, reseal, and turn to coat the fish completely. Refrigerate for 30 minutes, turning once.
3. Blanch, peel, and seed the tomatoes (see p. 100), and dice the remaining pulp.
4. Preheat the oven to 325°F (160°C). Drain the fillets and pat them dry with paper towels. Pick off any large chunks of garlic and discard, along with the marinade.

5. In a large, well-seasoned cast iron frying pan, heat 2 tablespoons (30 mL) olive oil on high and sear the fillets briefly on both sides. Transfer the fish to a shallow 9 × 13 (3.5 litre) glass baking dish. Add the onion to the frying pan, reduce the heat to medium-low, and sauté until transparent, about 3 minutes (do not brown). Stir in the garlic, oregano, thyme, and tomatoes; cover and simmer for about 5 minutes.

6. Pour the wine into the bottom of the baking dish, and then spoon the tomato mixture over the fillets. Bake, uncovered, until the fillets are opaque, about 10 minutes, depending on their thickness.

Pan-seared Halibut
with Mustard Dill Sauce

The mustard dill sauce in this recipe is nothing more than flavoured Béarnaise sauce. And it comes together exactly the same way as hollandaise: two incompatible liquids (melted butter and water) are blended together and held in place by an emulsifier (egg yolk—see p. 82 for tips on how emulsions work).

Mustard Dill Sauce

1. Take an extra egg out of the fridge and set it aside to come to room temperature. You may not need it, but having an extra egg yolk on hand can salvage your sauce if it "breaks" during cooking (see p. 82).
2. Prepare the double boiler: fill the bottom pan with enough water so that the top pan sits above the water, **not** in the water. Bring the water to a simmer, not a boil.
3. In a small saucepan, on medium heat, boil the wine vinegar with the shallot, the peppercorns, and the dill until the liquid is reduced to about ¼ cup (60 mL), between 3 and 5 minutes. Remove the reduction from the heat and allow to it cool so that it is warm, but no longer hot, between 3 and 4 minutes (if it is too hot, it will scramble the eggs). Strain the reduction through a fine sieve into the top of the double boiler.
4. In the same saucepan, melt the butter on low until just melted, but not hot.
5. In a small bowl, lightly beat the egg yolks and then whisk them into the vinegar reduction. Whisk until the mixture starts to thicken slightly, and then remove the double boiler from the heat.

Mustard Dill Sauce

⅓ cup (80 mL) white wine vinegar

2 shallots, minced

4 crushed peppercorns

2 Tbsp (30 mL) minced fresh dill

½ cup (125 mL) unsalted butter

2 large egg yolks, at room temperature

2 Tbsp (30 mL) grainy mustard

Halibut

4 5-oz (150 g) halibut fillets

½ tsp (2 mL) salt

freshly ground pepper, to taste

1 Tbsp (15 mL) extra virgin olive oil, for frying

1 Tbsp (15 mL) unsalted butter

2 Tbsp (30 mL) minced fresh dill, for garnishing

Serves 4.

Wine Suggestion: Chardonnay

6. Add the lukewarm butter, 1 tablespoon (15 mL) at a time, to the egg-yolk mixture, whisking constantly. Return the double boiler to the stove on low heat. When all the butter is incorporated and the sauce is thick, whisk in the mustard, 1 tablespoon (15 mL) at a time. Take the sauce off the heat and whisk occasionally while you broil the fish.

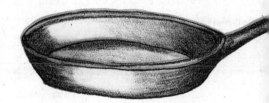

Halibut
1. Rinse the halibut and dry well with paper towels. Season both sides with salt and pepper. In a large, well-seasoned cast-iron frying pan, heat the oil and the butter on medium-high heat.
2. Estimate total cooking time for the fish at 10 minutes per inch 2.5 cm) of thickness. Add the fillets and sear on both sides until nicely browned, turning once about three-quarters of the way through the total cooking time, about 6 minutes, depending on their thickness.
3. Return the sauce to the heat for 1 minute, whisking constantly. Spoon the sauce onto 4 warm (but not hot) plates and top with a halibut fillet. Sprinkle each fillet with minced dill and serve immediately.

Halibut à l'Orange

This tangy orange sauce pairs wonderfully with meaty, firm-fleshed fish like halibut. For traditional Duck à l'Orange, the duck is cooked first and the sauce is started by deglazing the cooking pan. Due to the more fragile nature of fish, the halibut is cooked last for this recipe and the sauce is finished by deglazing the pan.

4 5-oz (150 g) skinless, boneless halibut fillets

½ tsp (2 mL) salt

freshly ground pepper, to taste

3 medium organic navel oranges

cold water in a bowl

2 Tbsp (30 mL) white vinegar

2 Tbsp (30 mL) white sugar

¼ cup (60 mL) unsalted butter, divided

2 Tbsp (30 mL) flour

1 cup (250 mL) Fish Stock (p. 160) (your choice, or substitute chicken stock)

1 Tbsp (15 mL) freshly squeezed lemon juice

4 tsp (20 mL) brandy

2 Tbsp (30 mL) Curaçao

Serves 4.

Wine Suggestion: Muscadet

1. Rinse the halibut fillets and dry with paper towels. Season both sides of each one with salt and pepper and set aside while you make the sauce.
2. Using a vegetable peeler, peel the rind from two of the oranges into long ribbons, about half an inch (1.25 cm) wide. Blanch the peels by boiling them in water for 3 minutes, and then plunge them immediately into the cold water. Drain and set aside.
3. In a small saucepan, cook the vinegar and the sugar on medium heat until the mixture turns a light brown, about 5 to 6 minutes.
4. In a second saucepan, melt 2 tablespoons (30 mL) butter and whisk in the flour. Cook for about 2 minutes, and then whisk in the stock.
5. Whisk the vinegar mixture into the stock mixture.
6. Squeeze the juice from all 3 oranges, and add the orange juice and the lemon juice to the stock mixture. Reduce the heat to low, and whisk occasionally while you cook the fish.

7. Pat the fish dry with paper towels to remove any moisture brought to the surface by the salt.

8. In a non-stick frying pan, heat the remaining 2 tablespoons (30 mL) butter on medium-high and let it brown. Add the halibut fillets and sauté for 5 minutes on the first side. Turn the fillets and drizzle 1 teaspoon (5 mL) of brandy over each one. Reduce the heat to medium and cook until the fish is opaque, about 3 minutes, depending on their thickness. Remove the halibut from the frying pan and place on 4 warmed plates.

9. Pour the orange sauce into the frying pan to deglaze the pan. Stir in the blanched orange peels and the Curaçao. Spoon a few ribbons of orange peel and a generous dollop of sauce over each fillet and serve immediately.

Baked Halibut
with Prawn Sauce

There are few things that are more rich and satisfying than seafood that is stuffed, sauced, or otherwise finished with other seafood; it's even better than dessert.

4 5-oz (150g) boneless, skinless halibut fillets

2 Tbsp (30 mL) olive oil

1 cup (250 mL) dry white wine

1 Tbsp (15 mL) unsalted butter, at room temperature

1 Tbsp (15 mL) flour

1 small onion, diced

2 garlic cloves, minced

½ tsp (2 mL) sea salt

freshly ground pepper, to taste

1 lb (500 g) raw prawns, shelled and de-veined

2 Tbsp (30 mL) minced flat-leaf parsley, for garnishing

Serves 4.

Wine Suggestion: Sémillon

1. Preheat the oven to 325°F (160°C). Rinse the halibut and pat it dry with paper towels.
2. In a large, non-stick frying pan, heat the olive oil on high and sear the fillets briefly on both sides.
3. Transfer the fish to a shallow 9 × 13 (3.5 litre) glass baking dish. Pour the wine into the bottom of the dish, cover with aluminum foil, and bake until the fish is opaque, about 10 minutes, depending on thickness.
4. Chop the prawns in half (in thirds, if they are large), and set aside. In a small bowl, use a small whisk to blend the flour into the butter, and set that aside, too.
5. Add the onion to the frying pan and cook on medium-low heat until it begins to caramelize, about 10 minutes. Add the garlic, salt, and pepper, and cook for 1 minute more (do not allow the garlic to brown).
6. Transfer the halibut to a warmed serving platter and keep the fillets warm in the oven (turn off the heat) while you finish the sauce.

7. Pour the liquid from the baking dish into the frying pan, bring it to a boil, and then reduce it by half. Lower the heat to medium and add the prawns.

8. Simmer the prawns until they are almost done, about 3 minutes, and then whisk in the butter/flour mixture. Continue to whisk until the sauce thickens and prawns are fully cooked, about 2 minutes more.

9. Spoon the prawn sauce over the halibut fillets, garnish with the parsley, and serve immediately.

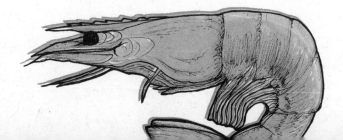

Balsamic Rosemary Halibut

Serve these fillets with a crusty loaf of bread and an oil-and-vinegar dip.

4 5-oz (150 g) halibut fillets

½ cup plus 2 Tbsp(155 mL) olive oil, divided

¼ cup (60 mL) balsamic vinegar

4 garlic cloves, peeled and squashed

4 sprigs fresh rosemary

1 tsp (5 mL) sea salt

freshly ground pepper, to taste

Serves 4.

Wine Suggestion: Chardonnay

1. Rinse the fish and pat it dry with paper towels.
2. In a heavy-duty, resealable freezer bag, mix ½ cup (125 mL) of the olive oil, vinegar, garlic, rosemary, salt, and pepper. Seal the bag and swish to combine the marinade ingredients. Add the halibut, seal the bag, and turn it a few times to coat the fish completely. Refrigerate for 30 minutes, turning once.
3. Remove the fillets from the bag and discard the marinade. Pick off any bits of garlic or rosemary off the fish and pat it dry with paper towels.
4. Preheat the broiler to high, grease a baking sheet with 1 teaspoon (5 mL) of the remaining olive oil and brush the rest of it onto both sides of the fish.
5. Grill the fillets close to broiler for a total cooking time of 10 minutes per inch of thickness, turning once. Cook slightly longer on the first side (about 6 minutes for a 1-inch [2.5 cm] thick fillet), and finish on the second side until the fish is just opaque.

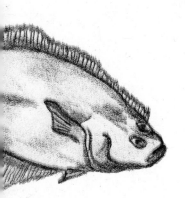

Cliffy's Notes

Originating in Italy, balsamic vinegar is technically not a wine vinegar, even though it is made from wine grapes. Freshly pressed grapes are not fermented initially but simply pressed and boiled until the juice is reduced by about one third. For traditional balsamic vinegar, the juice is then aged for up to 25 years in progressively smaller wooden barrels composed of a variety of woods. Needless to say, this makes for an extremely expensive product, and one that is protected by internal Italian regulations as well as by the European Union. As a result, most of us, myself included, have never tried the real thing.

Mass-produced balsamic vinegars are far more affordable, but they vary greatly in quality. The more expensive varieties are actual balsamic vinegar, made from reduced grape juice that has aged for about a year. The cheaper ones are not balsamic vinegars at all, but doctored wine vinegars that have been sweetened with sugar and darkened with caramel.

Pan-Seared Halibut
with Ginger Horseradish Crust

Fresh horseradish root is widely available in the produce department of many grocery stores, but if it you can't find it fresh in your area, use a hot, non-creamy bottled version for this halibut recipe.

Homemade Horseradish

1 cup (250 mL) peeled, diced fresh horseradish root

3 Tbsp (45 mL) white vinegar

1 tsp (5 mL) salt

Halibut

4 5-oz (150 g) boneless, skinless halibut fillets

2 Tbsp (30 mL) Homemade Horseradish (or substitute a hot, non-creamy bottled variety)

3 Tbsp (45 mL) finely grated fresh ginger

½ cup (250 mL) Panko breadcrumbs

½ tsp (2 mL) salt

freshly ground pepper, to taste

½ cup (125 mL) flour

2 eggs

4 Tbsp (60 mL) canola oil, divided

Serves 4.

Beer Suggestion: Cold ale

Homemade Horseradish

1. Put the horseradish and 3 tablespoons (45 mL) cold water in a food processor and process until smooth. Add the vinegar and salt, and process briefly to combine. (Store in an airtight glass jar in the freezer for up to 6 months.)

Halibut

1. Preheat the oven to 350°F (180°C). Rinse the halibut fillets, pat dry with paper towels, and set aside. In a wide, shallow bowl (a pasta bowl works well), combine the horseradish, ginger, breadcrumbs, salt, and pepper. In a second wide, shallow bowl, spread out the flour. In a third wide, shallow bowl, beat the eggs with a fork.

2. Dip the fillets first in flour, then in the egg, and last in the seasoned breadcrumb mixture. Set the fillets on a wire rack to dry for about 10 minutes.

3. In a large, non-stick frying pan, heat 2 tablespoons (30 mL) of the canola oil on high until it is very hot (but not smoking). Cooking the fillets 2 at a time (too much cold food in the pan can drop the temperature of the oil and the crust will not be crispy), sear both sides for a total cooking time of about 8 minutes, depending on their thickness. Keep the first 2 fillets warm in the oven while you cook the remaining fish, and then serve piping hot.

Panko Breadcrumbs

Panko is a kind of coarse Japanese breadcrumb that has become more widely available in Western supermarkets over the last few years. The crumbs are crunchier and lighter than traditional Western breadcrumbs, and they tend to absorb less oil, which makes them a popular choice for fried, breaded foods. (The crumbs are also bigger and flatter and resemble shredded coconut in appearance.)

Halibut Poached in Spicy Black Bean Sauce

Since I love the combination of black beans and chili oil, I buy black bean–chili paste in Chinatown; mixing a couple tablespoons (30 mL) of the chunky black bean sauce available at most grocery stores with a teaspoon (5 mL) of chili oil makes a good substitute.

2 Tbsp (30 mL) dry sherry

2 Tbsp (30 mL) dark soy sauce

1 tsp (5 mL) sugar

1 cup (250 mL) Fish Stock (p. 160) (your choice, or substitute chicken stock)

1 Tbsp (15 mL) cornstarch

¼ cup (60 mL) peanut oil, divided

2 garlic cloves, minced

3-inch (8 cm) piece fresh ginger, sliced thinly on the diagonal

2 Tbsp (30 mL) black bean–chili paste

4 5-oz (150 g) halibut fillets

4 green onions, sliced thinly on the diagonal

Serves 4.

Wine Suggestion: Riesling

1. In a small bowl, whisk together the sherry, soy sauce, sugar, Fish Stock, and cornstarch; set aside.
2. In a medium saucepan, heat 2 tablespoons (30 mL) of the peanut oil on high. Add the garlic, ginger, and black bean–chili paste and stir-fry for 2 to 3 minutes. Whisk in the sherry mixture and bring it to a boil. Reduce the heat to low and simmer, uncovered, for 10 minutes.
3. Rinse the fish and dry very well using paper towels. In a heavy-duty non-stick frying pan, heat the remaining peanut oil on high until very hot (but not smoking). Add the halibut and sear briefly on both sides.
4. Whisk the black bean mixture, and then pour it into the frying pan with the fish. Poach on a low simmer until the fillets are cooked through, about 2 minutes, depending on their thickness. Sprinkle with the green onion and serve immediately.

Leftovers

About Leftovers

We all have them: those little foil-wrapped science experiments at the back of the fridge—the leftover roast that we diligently put into a reusable container, and then forgot to date; the gelatinized stew with the skim of fat across the top, eyeing us balefully from the top shelf—silently screaming "eat me" every time we open the fridge.

So we close the door and pretend we didn't see them. We feel guilty about throwing out good food and our strategy seems to be to let it turn green because then we can toss it out in good conscience. Because, the truth is, figuring out what to do with leftovers can be more challenging than planning a whole new meal. It's tough to turn leftovers into something palatable, and if you have picky kids, well . . . sometimes it just seems like more effort than it's worth.

But it's an effort that we should make. The trash-can is indeed a dismal fate for any animal slaughtered for food, and tossing out a salmon fillet because we forgot about it, or grilling twice as much halibut as we can reasonably eat because we ran out of freezer bags, undermines the very tenets of sustainable fishing.

Seafood is a precious resource and the easiest steps we can take towards responsible ocean stewardship are to cook what we buy, and to eat what we cook.

On the lighter side, using up cold, leftover seafood is easier than it looks. With the exception of bivalves, which don't reheat all that well and are best turned into dips, most seafood can be reinvented into tomorrow's lunch in the form of savoury tarts, pâtés, quiches, and salads (and, in a pinch, even leftover mussels can be tossed into pasta sauce at the very last minute to "just heat through").

Dips

To store leftover clams and mussels, remove the meat from the shells and refrigerate in a covered container for use the following day in a cream cheese–based dip. This is not only fast and easy, but it also side-steps the problem of reheating, which tends to make previously cooked bivalves somewhat rubbery. I particularly like serving these dips with crispy Asian crackers.

Clam Dip

1 cup (250 mL) shucked leftover clams
4 oz (120 g) cream cheese, softened
1 Tbsp (15 mL) Worcestershire sauce
1 Tbsp (15 mL) Dijon mustard
¼ cup (60 mL) whipping cream
2 Tbsp (30 mL) minced green onion

Horseradish Mussel Dip

1 cup (250 mL) shucked leftover mussels
4 oz (120 g) cream cheese, softened
½ cup (125 mL) cottage cheese
1 Tbsp (15 mL) freshly squeezed lemon juice
1 Tbsp (15 mL) horseradish
1 Tbsp (15 mL) Worcestershire sauce
½ tsp (2 mL) salt
freshly ground pepper, to taste
¼ tsp (1 mL) cayenne pepper
4 green onions, finely chopped

Clam Dip

1. Mince the clams and set them aside. Whisk together the cream cheese, Worcestershire sauce, mustard, and whipping cream, and then fold in the minced clams and green onion. Cover and refrigerate for 1 to 2 hours to allow the flavours to blend.

Horseradish Mussel Dip

1. For this dip, either use Homemade Horseradish (p. 140), or use a hot, non-creamy bottled variety.
2. Mince the mussels and set aside. In a food processor, blend the cream cheese, cottage cheese, lemon juice, horseradish, Worcestershire sauce, salt, pepper, and cayenne and process until smooth. Transfer this mixture to a serving bowl and fold in the mussels and green onion. Cover and chill for 1 to 2 hours before serving.

Salmon and New Potato Salad

Pair your leftover salmon with freshly boiled new potatoes and lemon vinaigrette, and serve this salad in individual lettuce cups for a delicious weekend lunch.

1. Add all the ingredients for the vinaigrette to a screw-top jar and shake well.
2. Rinse the potatoes, being careful not to damage or strip off the skins. Boil them whole in a large pan of salted water. Drain, cover, and refrigerate until cold, at least 30 minutes.
3. When the potatoes are chilled, add the celery, pepper, cucumber, green onion, and Lemon Vinaigrette to the potatoes and stir well to combine. Cover and marinate in the fridge for another 30 minutes.
4. Pick over the salmon for bones and break it into bite-size pieces (do not crumble it). Add it to the potatoes and stir to combine. To serve, line salad bowls with large iceberg lettuce leaves and spoon the potato salad directly onto the lettuce.

Lemon Vinaigrette

¼ cup (60 mL) lemon juice

¾ cup (185 mL) extra virgin olive oil

½ tsp (2 mL) mustard powder

½ tsp (2 mL) dried basil

½ tsp (2 mL) dried marjoram

½ tsp (2 mL) salt

freshly ground pepper, to taste

Salmon Potato Salad

1 lb (500 g) new red potatoes
(the smallest ones you can find)

½ cup (125 mL) chopped celery

½ cup (125 mL) chopped red bell pepper

½ cup (125 mL) chopped
long English cucumber

3 Tbsp (45 mL) chopped green onion

1 lb (500 g) leftover salmon, cold

iceberg lettuce leaves, for serving

Serves 4.

Wine Suggestion: Chardonnay

Seafood Cannelloni

Fresh pasta sheets are widely available in grocery stores, making cannelloni a snap to make. Their shorter cooking time ensures that your leftover seafood doesn't get tough and rubbery in the oven, and rolling the pasta sheets around the filling is a lot easier than trying to stuff preformed tubes.

Seafood Filling

Seafood Filling

2 Tbsp (30 mL) unsalted butter
1 shallot, minced
1 cup (250 mL) chopped, cooked prawns
1 cup (250 mL) chopped, cooked crabmeat
½ tsp (2 mL) salt
freshly ground pepper, to taste
(white, if you have it)

1. In a medium frying pan, melt the butter on medium-high heat and sauté the shallot until transparent, about 2 minutes (do not brown). Remove pan from heat and allow the mixture to cool slightly before stirring in the prawns, crabmeat, salt, and pepper.

Herb Sauce

Herb Sauce

2 Tbsp (30 mL) unsalted butter
2 Tbsp (30 mL) flour
½ cup (125 mL) milk
½ cup (125 mL) cream
1 tsp (5 mL) minced fresh fennel fronds
1 tsp (5 mL) minced fresh tarragon
1 tsp (5 mL) minced chives

1. In a small saucepan, melt the butter on medium heat and whisk in the flour. Cook until the mixture is fragrant, about 2 minutes, but do not allow the flour to brown. Gradually whisk in the milk and bring to a simmer. Whisk in the cream and the fresh herbs and set aside, uncovered.

Seafood Cannelloni

1. Preheat the oven to 350°F (180°C). Par-cook all the pasta sheets prior to filling them: in a large pot of salted water, boil the pasta sheets 2 at a time, for about 2 minutes. Remove with a slotted spoon and drain briefly on a tea towel. Transfer the pasta to a solid work surface and spoon approximately ¼ cup (60 mL) of the Seafood Filling onto each cannelloni, lining it along one edge of the pasta sheet. Starting with the stuffed side, roll the pasta around the filling, leaving the ends open.

2. Grease 4 individual baking dishes with the melted butter, and place 2 cannelloni, seam side down, in each one. Spoon a quarter of the Herb Sauce into each dish and bake until the sauce is bubbling and the seafood is heated through, about 10 minutes.

3. Mix together the remaining minced herbs and sprinkle a pinch over each dish after removing from the oven. Serve on a large plate or on a heatproof placemat.

Seafood Cannelloni

fresh pasta sheets, cut to into 8 pieces that are 6 × 4 inches (15 × 10 cm) each

1 recipe Seafood Filling (p. 146)

2 Tbsp (30 mL) melted butter, for greasing

1 recipe Herb Sauce (p. 146)

1 tsp (5 mL) each minced fresh fennel, tarragon, and chives for garnishing

Serves 4.

Wine Suggestion: Sauvignon Blanc

Salmon Pâté

Pâté is a perfect way to use up leftover salmon and this recipe is particularly flexible: simply keep the salmon and cream cheese in proportion, and increase or decrease the blue cheese and seasonings accordingly. Serve with crackers or toasted baguette rounds.

3 garlic cloves
2 Tbsp (30 mL) unsalted butter
½ lb (250 g) cooked salmon, cold
1 Tbsp (15 mL) freshly squeezed lemon juice
1 tsp (5 mL) Worcestershire sauce
1 8-oz (250 g) package cream cheese, at room temperature
¼ cup (60 mL) blue cheese, crumbled
½ tsp (2 mL) salt
freshly ground pepper, to taste
1 Tbsp (15 mL) whipping cream (optional)
3 green onions, minced, divided
2 Tbsp (30 mL) melted butter, for brushing
Serves 12 as buffet finger food.

1. Squash the garlic cloves with the side of a large chef's knife to pop them out of their skins, and then squash them a few more times to release their oil. Place the garlic and the butter in a small glass measuring cup and microwave on low until the butter melts. Pick out and discard the garlic, and set the butter aside to cool to room temperature.
2. Use a fork to flake the salmon, removing any bones and skin. Place the fish in a food processor with the lemon juice and Worcestershire sauce and process until smooth. Add the garlic butter, cream cheese, blue cheese, salt, and pepper, and process until smooth. If the pâté seems too thick, blend in the whipping cream.
3. Transfer the pâté to a serving bowl and fold in half the green onion. Smooth the top with a rubber spatula, cover with plastic wrap and refrigerate for 30 minutes. When the pâté is chilled, brush the top with the melted butter to seal, and garnish with the remaining green onion.

Fish Cakes

While many fish cake recipes call for boiled, mashed potatoes, I find cooking the potatoes in water results in a wet, pasty texture. I prefer to microwave them and break them up with a fork or a potato ricer once they're cool enough to handle.

1. Microwave the potatoes until you can pierce them easily with a fork, 5 to 10 minutes, depending on your microwave, and set aside to cool. When they are cool enough to handle, scoop the insides into a large mixing bowl and mash roughly with a fork (they will be easier to mash if they are still slightly warm). Mash in the butter, garlic, green onion, salt, and pepper.

2. Use a fork to flake the fish into a small bowl, removing any skin and bones. In a small mixing bowl, lightly beat the eggs with the Worcestershire sauce and the mustard. Stir the egg mixture into the fish, and then fold the fish mixture into the potatoes.

3. Spread the flour on a large plate. Press the fish mixture into small patties and dip both sides in the flour, shaking off any excess.

4. In a well-seasoned cast-iron frying pan, heat the canola oil on high heat until hot (but not smoking). Pan-fry the fish cakes until they are golden brown and heated through, about 2 to 3 minutes per side, depending on thickness. Serve with Tartar Sauce (p. 24), lemon wedges, and extra Worcestershire sauce on the side.

2 large russet potatoes
2 Tbsp (30 mL) butter
2 garlic cloves, finely minced
3 green onions, finely minced
½ tsp (2 mL) salt
freshly ground pepper, to taste
1 lb (500 g) cold halibut
2 eggs
1 Tbsp (15 mL) Worcestershire sauce
1 tsp (5 mL) Dijon mustard
½ cup (125 mL) flour
3 Tbsp (45 mL) canola oil
2 lemons, cut into wedges
Serves 4 for lunch.

Beer Suggestion: Cold ale

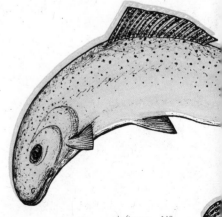

Salmon Fritters

Seafood fritters differ from other battered fish recipes only in the ratio of fish to batter. Instead of coating a large piece of raw fish with a thin layer of batter, to make a fritter, small bits of cooked fish are suspended within a seasoned batter, which is dropped by the spoonful into hot oil. You don't need much salmon for this recipe so it's handy if you only have a single leftover fillet to use up.

Batter

1 cup (250 mL) flour
1 tsp (5 mL) baking powder
1 tsp (5 mL) salt
freshly ground pepper, to taste
1 Tbsp (15 mL) canolo oil
¾ cup (185 mL) milk
2 eggs, separated into yolks and whites, divided

Fritter Batter

1 cup (250 mL) chopped, cooked salmon, chilled
1 jalapeno pepper, minced (optional)
¼ cup (60 mL) minced red bell pepper
¼ cup (60 mL) minced green onion
½ cup (125 mL) canola oil, for frying
Serves 4.

Wine Suggestion: Sémillon

1. In a medium mixing bowl, sift the flour with the baking powder, salt, and pepper. In a second bowl, lightly beat the egg yolks, and then whisk canola oil and the milk. Stir the wet ingredients into the dry ingredients and mix until just combined (do not overmix). Cover and refrigerate for at least an hour.

2. Stir the salmon, peppers, and green onion into the chilled batter. Set aside.

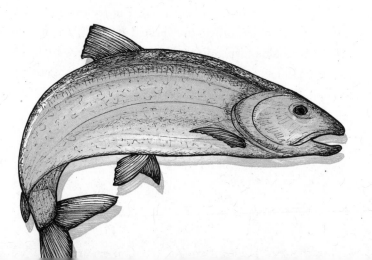

3. In a separate medium bowl, whip the egg whites into stiff peaks. Just before frying, fold them into the batter.

4. In a large frying pan (or use your deep fryer, paying close attention to the manufacturer's maximum fill line), heat canola oil on high until very hot (but not smoking). Drop tablespoonfuls (15 mL) of batter into the oil, cooking the fritters a few at a time (overloading your pan will reduce the temperature of the oil and the fritters will be oily), until golden brown, about 3 to 4 minutes (if not using a deep fryer, turn once halfway through cooking). Drain on paper towels and serve piping hot with fresh lemon wedges and coarsely ground sea salt.

Crab-stuffed Crepes

This elegant brunch dish is an easy way to use up the body meat leftover from other crab recipes that focus on the legs and claws, such as Chilled Marinated Crab Legs (p. 24). Make the crepes an hour or two ahead of time, and stack them, unrefrigerated, in between sheets of wax paper. Add colour to your presentation with a garnish of fresh herbs, or serve crepes with a vibrant fruit salad.

Crepes

2 large eggs

1 cup (250 mL) milk

1 cup (250 mL) all-purpose flour

3 Tbsp (45 mL) melted butter, for brushing

Crab Filling

2 Tbsp (30 mL) unsalted butter

1 shallot, minced

2 Tbsp (30 mL) flour

¼ cup (60 mL) dry sherry

1 cup (250 mL) milk

½ cup (125 mL) whipping cream

⅛ tsp (0.5 mL) grated nutmeg

⅛ tsp (0.5 mL) cayenne pepper

¼ tsp (1 mL) salt

freshly ground pepper, to taste (white, if you have it)

1 lb (500 g), cooked crabmeat, cooled and picked over for shells

Serves 4.

Wine Suggestion: Champagne

Crepes

1. In a large mixing bowl, lightly beat the eggs, and then whisk in the milk. Whisk in the flour and beat until the batter is smooth. If time allows, let the batter rest for about an hour before frying.

2. Brush a medium, non-stick frying pan on medium heat with a thin layer of melted butter. Pour in ¼ cup (60 mL) of batter and tilt the pan so the batter covers the bottom of the pan in a thin, even layer. Cook the first side until the crepe starts to brown at the edges, about 3 minutes. Turn the crepe using a rubber spatula and cook the second side for another minute. Set the crepe on a plate and cover with a sheet of wax paper. Repeat until all the batter is used. (You should have 8 to 10 crepes.)

Crab Filling

1. In a medium saucepan, melt the butter on medium heat and cook the shallot until translucent, about 4 minutes. Whisk in the flour and cook until the flour starts to brown, about 2 minutes. Whisk in the sherry, and then gradually add the milk. Bring the mixture to a simmer and whisk until the sauce thickens slightly, about 3 to 4 minutes

2. Add the whipping cream, nutmeg, cayenne, salt, and pepper. Reduce the heat to medium-low and simmer for another 5 minutes, and then stir in the crab. When the crab is heated through, about 1 to 2 minutes, divide the crab filling evenly between the crepes—either rolling the crepe around the filling, or setting the filling in the top righthand quarter of the crepe, folding the crepe in half, and then folding it in half again to make a fan shape. Serve warm.

Cliffy's Notes

Dungeness crabs are encased in a hard exoskeleton that does not expand to accommodate the animal growing inside. When a crab outgrows its shell (about 6 or 7 times a year for young crabs, less frequently for larger crabs), the crab cracks its own shell at the rear, and then backs out, leaving the old shell behind. At this point, the crab is considered a "soft shell" crab, because its new exoskeleton is very thin and pliable soft (at this point, non-Dungeness "soft shell" crabs are harvested for the kitchen and deep-fried whole).

The freshly molted crab then absorbs water and puffs itself up to more than half again its regular size while the new shell hardens, which takes about three days. Once the new shell hardens, the crab expels the water, which is why a newly molted crab will feel light for its size and be a disappointing size on your plate.

Salmon Potato Skins

I make Salmon Potato Skins on those happy days when I have both leftover salmon *and* leftover baked potatoes—but you can, of course, make them from scratch.

½ lb (250 g) leftover salmon, boned and skinned

2 large baked potatoes, skins on

2 Tbsp (30 mL) unsalted butter, at room temperature

1 Tbsp (15 mL) Worcestershire sauce

1 garlic clove, minced

2 green onions, minced

½ tsp (2 mL) salt

freshly ground pepper, to taste

½ cup (125 mL) grated sharp cheddar cheese

Serves 4 as an appetizer, or 2 for lunch.

Beer Suggestion: Cold ale

1. Preheat the oven to 350°F (180°C). If you are starting with cold potatoes that have been refrigerated, warm them for a few seconds in the microwave, which will make it easier to scoop out the potato. Being careful not to tear the skins, cut the potatoes lengthwise and scoop the insides into a mixing bowl. Reserve the skins.
2. Add the butter, Worcestershire sauce, garlic, green onion, salt, and pepper to the potato and mash it to a smooth consistency using a fork.
3. Use a fork to flake the salmon and fold it into the potato mixture. Mound the salmon/potato mixture into the potato skins and top each one with about 2 tablespoons (30 mL) of the grated cheddar. Bake until heated through, about 10 minutes, and then switch the oven to broil to brown the tops, cooking for 1 to 2 minutes more. Serve piping hot with extra Worcestershire sauce on the side.

Crab and Chanterelle Tarts

Available fresh in late summer and early fall, these wild gourmet mushrooms are a true culinary treat.

1. Preheat the oven to 400°F (200°C). Defrost the puff pastry according to package directions and set aside.
2. In a medium mixing bowl, whisk the whipping cream into the cream cheese. Stir in the garlic, green onion, cayenne pepper, salt, and pepper, and then gently fold in the crabmeat and chopped mushrooms.
3. Bake the empty pastry shells according to the package directions. Remove the shells from the oven and divide the crab mixture equally between them. Sprinkle the tops with the Parmesan cheese and bake until the crab mixture is heated through, about 5 minutes more. Switch the oven to broil and grill briefly until the cheese is golden brown.

4 large frozen puff pastry shells

2 Tbsp (30 mL) whipping cream

¾ cup (185 mL) cream cheese, at room temperature

2 garlic cloves, minced

2 Tbsp (30 mL) minced green onion

½ tsp (2 mL) cayenne pepper

½ tsp (2 mL) salt

freshly ground pepper, to taste

½ lb (250 g) cooked Dungeness crabmeat

½ lb (250 g) fresh chanterelle mushrooms, chopped

½ cup (125 mL) freshly grated Parmesan cheese

Serves 4.

Wine Suggestion: Unoaked Chardonnay

Salmon Quiche

Quiche is an open, savoury pie traditionally made with bread dough as a crust. Modern versions have replaced the bread dough with short-crust pastry (think apple pie), or puff pastry (think apple turnovers). And, for those who prefer pie pastry, I have included a recipe below that works well with egg-based pie fillings.

Crust

1. Sift the flours into a chilled mixing bowl. Using a pastry blender or two butter knives, cut the chilled butter and shortening into the flour. When all the fat is about the size of peas, use your fingertips to work it into the flour to obtain a uniform crumbly mixture (alternately, you could use a stand mixer).

2. Gradually mix in the salted water until the flour forms a ball. If the mixture seems dry, add another teaspoon (5 mL) or so of water. Flatten the ball into a disc, wrap it in plastic, and refrigerate for 30 minutes.

3. Preheat the oven to 400°F (200°C). On a cold, lightly floured surface, roll the chilled pastry into an 11-inch (28 cm) circle and press it into an ungreased 9-inch (23 cm) fluted tart pan and trim the edge. Cut a piece of parchment paper to fit inside the bottom of the pan and weigh it down with a layer of pastry weights (or dried legumes) about 1 inch (2.5 cm) thick. Put the pan in the fridge for about 10 minutes, and then bake the chilled pastry for 15 minutes while you prepare the filling.

4. Take the par-baked crust out of the oven. Remove the pastry weights and parchment paper and prick the crust all over with a fork. Brush the pastry with the beaten egg to seal it. Bake for another 5 minutes, remove from the oven, and set aside.

Salmon Quiche

1. In a medium frying pan, melt the butter on medium heat and sauté the shallot and parsley until fragrant, about 2 minutes (do not brown). Stir in the lemon juice, salt, and pepper. Pick over the salmon for any stray bones, and then crumble it and stir it into the shallot mixture. Remove pan from heat and set aside.

2. In a medium mixing bowl, whisk the cream into the mascarpone and the cream cheese, and then add the beaten eggs a third at a time.

3. Spread the salmon mixture evenly across the bottom of the pie crust. Pour the egg mixture over the salmon and spread it to an even thickness.

4. Set the quiche on the centre rack of the oven and reduce the heat immediately to 300°F (150°C). Bake until the eggs are set and the top is golden brown, about 35 to 40 minutes. Let the quiche set for about 5 minutes prior to slicing. May be served hot or chilled.

Baking Tip

If you prefer puff pastry, buy it frozen and follow the directions on the package.

Salmon Quiche

2 Tbsp (30 mL) unsalted butter

1 shallot, minced

2 Tbsp (30 mL) minced fresh flat-leaf parsley

1 Tbsp (15 mL) freshly squeezed lemon juice

1 tsp (5 mL) salt

freshly ground pepper, to taste

½ lb (250 grams) salmon, skin and bones removed

½ cup (125 mL) light cream (10% milkfat)

½ cup (125 mL) mascarpone cheese, at room temperature

½ cup (125 mL) cream cheese, at room temperature

3 eggs, lightly beaten

1 prebaked crust (p. 156)

Serves 4.

Wine Suggestion: Unoaked Chardonnay

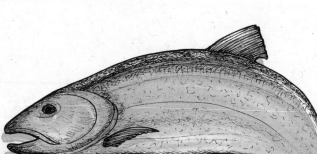

Salmon Puffs with Caper Sauce

This is an easy egg-leavened dish that makes a great family lunch when you don't have the time or the inclination to face the drama of a bona fide soufflé. Make the sauce while the salmon puffs are baking.

Salmon Puffs

2 Tbsp (30 mL) butter, at room temperature, for greasing

2 cups (500 mL) flaked, cooked salmon, chilled and picked over for bones

2 Tbsp (30 mL) melted butter

3 green onions, minced

½ cup (125 mL) dried breadcrumbs

1 egg and 2 egg whites, divided (reserve 1 egg yolk for Caper Sauce)

¼ cup (60 mL) milk

¼ cup (60 mL) whipping cream

Serves 4.

Wine Suggestion: Sémillon

Salmon Puffs

1. Preheat the oven to 350°F (180°C). Grease 4 ramekins (1 cup [250 mL] capacity) with butter.
2. In a medium mixing bowl, stir together the salmon, melted butter, green onion, and breadcrumbs.
3. In a small mixing bowl, lightly beat 1 egg, and then whisk in the milk and whipping cream. Add this mixture to the salmon and stir to combine.
4. In a clean bowl, use an electric mixer to beat the 2 egg whites until they form stiff peaks. Fold the egg whites into the salmon mixture, and then portion it into the ramekins. Set them on a baking sheet placed onto the centre rack of the oven and increase the heat immediately to 375°F (190°C). Bake until the eggs are puffed and set, about 20 minutes.

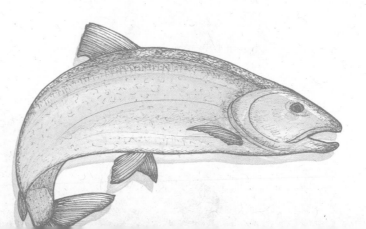

Caper Sauce

1. In a small saucepan, melt 2 tablespoons (30 mL) of the butter on medium heat and whisk in the flour. Cook the mixture until the flour starts to brown, about 2 to 3 minutes.

2. Whisk in the stock, bring to a high simmer and reduce the liquid to about 1½ cups (375 mL). Remove the mixture from the heat.

3. In a small bowl, beat the egg yolk with the cream and the nutmeg. When the stock reduction has cooled for 3 to 4 minutes, whisk the egg mixture into the stock (the temperature of the stock must be less than 180°F (82°C) when you add it to the egg or the yolks will scramble; use a candy thermometer if you're worried).

4. Return the saucepan to the stove and whisk in the capers on low heat. Ladle sauce over Salmon Puffs and serve.

Caper Sauce

3 Tbsp (45 mL) unsalted butter, divided

2 Tbsp (30 mL) flour

2 cups (500 mL) Fish Stock (p. 160), (your choice, or substitute chicken stock)

1 egg yolk (saved from making Salmon Puffs)

2 Tbsp (30 mL) whipping cream

⅛ tsp (0.5 mL) nutmeg

1 Tbsp (15 mL) chopped capers

Fish Stocks

Save prawn heads, fish heads, crab shells, fish bones, and other trimmings to make stock. Using a white fish stock, also called "fumet," adds subtlety to sauces and soups, making it less likely to overpower the seafood it accompanies. When making stock, it is important never to boil the water, as the heat and agitation will break down the protein and fat in the fish and leave you with cloudy, unappetizing goop, not clear broth.

White Fish Stock (Fumet)

White Fish Stock (Fumet)

2 lb (1 kg) raw fish trimmings (heads, bones, etc.)
2 Tbsp (30 mL) canola oil
1 stalk celery, thickly sliced
1 small onion, chopped
1 cup (250 mL) dry white wine
1 bay leaf
1 sprig fresh thyme

Prawn Stock

2 Tbsp (30 mL) canola oil
1 small onion, chopped
1 small fennel bulb, chopped
2 lb (1 kg) prawn heads
2 sprigs fresh thyme

Crab Stock

2 Tbsp (30 mL) canola oil
1 leek, chopped
1 celery stalk, thickly sliced
2 garlic cloves, peeled and squashed
2 lb (1 kg) cooked crab shells
2 bay leaves
1 sprig fresh thyme
1 tsp (5 mL) cracked black peppercorns

White Fish Stock (Fumet)

1. Rinse the bones to remove any traces of blood, which will turn the stock cloudy. In a large stockpot on medium-low heat, heat the oil and cook the celery, onion, and fish trimmings until the onion is translucent, 3 or 4 minutes (do not brown).
2. Add the wine, bring it to a simmer and reduce the liquid by half, about 5 minutes. Add the bay leaf and the thyme, and enough water to cover the fish bones (approximately 8 cups [2 L] of water for 2 lb [1 kg] of trimmings). Bring back to a simmer and cook for about 20 minutes, skimming off any foam that rises to the surface.
3. Cool the stock, and then strain it through a fine sieve, discarding the trimmings and vegetables. Transfer to an airtight container and refrigerate for up to 3 days (or freeze for up to 3 months). Makes about 8 cups (2 L).

Prawn Stock

1. In a large stockpot, heat the oil on medium heat and cook the onion and fennel until transparent, about 3 minutes. Add the prawn heads and the thyme, and enough water to cover them (about 8 cups [2 L] water for 2 lb [1 kg] prawn heads). Simmer for 1 hour, skimming off any foam that rises to the surface.

2. Cool the stock, and then strain it through a fine sieve, discarding the prawn heads and vegetables. Transfer to an airtight container and refrigerate for up to 3 days (or freeze for up to 3 months). Makes about 8 cups (2 L).

Crab Stock

1. In a large stockpot, heat the oil on medium heat, and cook the leek, celery, and garlic until transparent, about 3 minutes. Add the crab shells (you may need to break them to make them fit in the stockpot), bay leaves, thyme, and peppercorns, and enough cold water to cover everything (about 8 cups [2 L] for 2 lb [1 kg] of crab shells. Simmer for 1 hour, skimming off any foam that rises to the surface.

2. Cool the stock, and then strain it through a fine sieve, discarding the crab shells and vegetables. Transfer to an airtight container and refrigerate for up to 3 days (or freeze for up to 3 months). Makes about 8 cups (2 L).

Sourcing Fresh Fish Trimmings

Crab shells are the easiest to come by, and, in lieu of fresh prawn heads, you can save prawn shells in the freezer until you have enough. Some fishmongers will sell you fresh trimmings for next to nothing, or you can buy small, inexpensive whole fish for making stock. In a pinch, you can even substitute bottled clam juice.

Salmon Fried Rice

While this recipe is a far cry from a traditional Asian stir-fry, the spices and the shiitake mushrooms pair well with the salmon, making this colourful dish a tasty way to use up a leftover fillet or two.

4 Tbsp (60 mL) sesame oil, divided

¾ cup (185 mL) uncooked basmati rice

2 garlic cloves, minced

2 Tbsp (30 mL) dark soy sauce

2 Tbsp (30 mL) oyster sauce

1 tsp (5 mL) hot chili oil

1 tsp (5 mL) cornstarch

1 lb (500 g) cooked salmon, skinned and boned, cold

2 cups (500 mL) chopped shiitake mushrooms

1 4-inch (10 cm) piece fresh ginger, sliced thinly on the diagonal

1 red bell pepper, julienned

4 green onions, sliced on the diagonal

Serves 2.

Wine Suggestion: Gewürztraminer

1. In a medium saucepan, heat 2 tablespoons (30 mL) of the sesame oil on medium and sauté the rice until translucent, about 4 minutes. Add the garlic and sauté until fragrant, about 2 minutes (do not brown). Add enough cold water to cover the rice by half an inch (1.25 cm) and bring to a boil. Reduce the heat to low and simmer until all the water has been absorbed. Cover and turn off the heat, but leave the pot on the stove to keep warm.

2. In a small mixing bowl, whisk together the soy sauce, oyster sauce, hot chili oil, and cornstarch. Break up the salmon into bite-size chunks and pick it over for any bones.

3. In a large, well-seasoned cast-iron frying pan, heat the remaining 2 tablespoons (30 mL) of sesame oil on high and sauté the mushrooms and the ginger until the mushrooms release their liquid, about 4 minutes, and then add the cooked rice. Add the soy sauce mixture and stir well to coat the rice. Stir in the salmon and the red pepper and cook until the fish is heated through and the red pepper is tender-crisp, 3 or 4 minutes. Stir in the green onion and serve.

Index

Acknowledgments

First thanks go to my husband, Ted, who has supported me through many whacky adventures for more than sixteen years, believing in me long before I learned to believe in myself. If not for his love and encouragement, this book would still be a pile of grease-spattered notes in the kitchen drawer.

To my son, Gabriel, who ferried coffee (or wine, depending on how it was going), to my study during the writing process, and to my daughter, Jessica, who inquired with genuine compassion whether I was "nearly done my homework."

To my sister, Freya Lee, for reading the first draft and succinctly pointing out that I've never met an adjective I didn't like; had I sent the original ten-pound manuscript, it probably would have been met with a rejection letter.

To my mother, Ann Hory, for her unlimited encouragement and her help with the recipes; my father, Frank Hory, for teaching me to fish all those years ago; and to my brother, Andrew James, who always helped me to pull up the crab traps, even though he's a staunch vegetarian.

To Debbie Harding for her illustrations.

Special thanks go to Ruth Linka, for taking a chance on an unknown writer—particularly an unknown writer who isn't even a qualified chef—and for her patience and generosity of spirit in introducing a first-time author to the publishing industry.

To Holland Gidney, for her insightful editing, gentle correction, and especially her warm words of encouragement early in the process.

To Pete Kohut, for his great design and remarkable ability in getting the manuscript to fit the space.

And to Tara Saracuse, for her encouragement, lightning fast emails, great advice, and unflagging efforts in promoting this book.

It's been a steep learning curve, and I've enjoyed every minute.

Go Nuts: Recipes that Really Shell Out
Debbie Harding

978-1-926741-11-6 • $19.95

Brie and Walnut Stuffed Figs
Pumpkin Pecan Pancakes
Honey Almond Spread

Just a few of the extraordinary nut-themed dishes from
Go Nuts, the first cookbook to feature an all-nut cast of
culinary delight.